MW00472963

Divine Mercy and Divine Justice:

Why Both are Essential to a Catholic Understanding of God

Robert Stackpole, STD

Published by Thomas D. Hamel
"The Chartwell Press"
thechartwellpress.com

Copyright © 2020 Robert Stackpole
Printed in the United States of America
All Rights Reserved
ISBN 978-0-9919880-8-2

For Frank and Angelina
With Affection and Gratitude

Table of Contents

Foreword

This is an excellent and much needed book. It carefully and clearly addresses some of the biggest confusions common in the church today concerning such important topics as the reality of Heaven, Hell and Purgatory and how to understand the relation between God's mercy and God's justice. Misunderstanding revealed truth on these important topics is not just an academic problem: it jeopardizes salvation itself as well as undermining the call to holiness and evangelization and the motivation for anyone to dedicate their life to the service of God and his people.

Let me share an experience I had that illustrates the point. One day I was speaking to a group about what Jesus teaches about the danger of unrepented serious sin separating us from God forever and a woman came up to me afterwards and declared boldly: "My Jesus would never have said that."

Shocking. Troubling. Not many people today go around carving little wooden statues and worshipping them but many people today do go around picking and choosing what they like and don't like in the teaching of Jesus and the Church. It can be a form of idolatry and profound rebellion, creating a "god" in our own image and making up our own religion because we find "offensive" the real Jesus and his actual teaching.

How important is that all of us carefully pay attention to what God has revealed about himself and the way to salvation and how the Church has understood this and faithfully transmitted it all these years until it is summed up today in the Catechism of the Catholic Church.

Dr. Stackpole blends together the results of careful reasoning and sensitive attention to the revelation of God, and addresses in a way that may help many with the huge deceptions that are weakening the faith, morality and mission of God's people today.

Although the book is academically sound it is written in such a way that the educated Catholic can certainly understand the flow of his argument and greatly benefit from it.

His treatment of the truth about God's mercy and justice is absolutely essential for understanding who God is and how we should respond to him.

He has devoted whole chapters to the important topics of Purgatory and Hell and does not shrink from dealing with the "soft universalism" of Hans Urs Von Balthasar, Cardinal Kasper, and Bishop Barron which he demonstrates is not solidly grounded in the true faith of the church or in reason.

He addresses the tough questions: "If God is so merciful, why is there a hell?" "Why was the horrible death of Jesus Christ by crucifixion necessary for our salvation?" "Why do we shy away from facing the truth of the need for punishment – the penal dimension – for our sins?"

In the course of the book he has many occasions to show how the revelations made to St. Faustina about Divine Mercy, also include clear and repeated warnings that God's mercy is not forced on anyone but it must be accepted in humility and lead to repentance and conversion.

In a final chapter he does a masterful job of showing the relevance of mercy to Catholic social teaching.

This is a book that was written with careful attention to the truth and a deep concern for the salvation of souls. It is also a book that took courage to write and for that we are all in Dr. Stackpole's debt.

Ralph Martin, STD
President of Renewal Ministries in Ann Arbor, Michigan
Director of graduate programs in the New Evangelization at Sacred Heart Seminary in Detroit

Chapter One
God of Mercy, or Justice — or Both?

If you ask Catholics devoted to the Divine Mercy why they find the message and devotion so helpful, often they will tell you, "Because it helped me see that God is not a God of wrath and anger, but the One who loves us all with great mercy and compassion."

On the other hand, if you ask many "traditionalist" Catholics what they object to about the Divine Mercy devotion, often they will say: "It distorts Catholic doctrine about God, because it says that He is a God of mercy only, and not also a God of justice."

These two perspectives have something very significant in common: They are both wrong.

As the director of the John Paul II Institute of Divine Mercy, a post which I have held for over 20 years, I meet people with these misunderstandings all the time. For example, a while back someone pointed out to me an article on a traditionalist website that claimed that the revelations given to St. Maria Faustina Kowalska (1905-1938), the great Apostle of Divine Mercy, are actually *heretical*, because they offer us "complete remission of sins and punishment" on Divine Mercy Sunday without the requirement of penance and perfect contrition for sin. This is unheard of in Catholic Tradition, they said, and it violates the justice of God.

It's not, and it doesn't.

In any adult Baptism, the soul is washed clean with the complete remission of sins and punishment even if the soul is in a state of imperfect sorrow and repentance for sin. And this is not a violation of Divine Justice. As St. Thomas Aquinas tells us in his *Scriptum super Sententias* (d.2, q.1, quaes. 2), since in Baptism we are baptized into the death of Christ (as St. Paul teaches in his Epistle to the Romans chapter 6), the baptized person receives the full effects of Christ's Passion and Death. In other words, on the basis of His sacrifice on the Cross, in baptism our Lord completely remits our sins and all the punishment due to them.[1]

And yet, the traditionalists are definitely right about one thing: The Catholic Faith holds that God is both perfect in justice and perfect in mercy, at one and the same time. This truth of the faith is all too often ignored in the Church today, but it is the clear teaching of Holy Scripture, Sacred Tradition, the *Catechism of the Catholic Church*, and the revelations received by St. Faustina, as recorded in her *Diary*. In fact, as I hope to show in this series, without a proper understanding of the justice of God, we cannot fully appreciate His Divine Mercy either.

To begin with, we need to be clear by what we mean by the terms "Divine Mercy" and "Divine Justice."

For a definition of Divine Mercy, I am going to quote here what I wrote in my book *Divine Mercy: A Guide from Genesis to Benedict XVI*:

Divine Mercy is God's love reaching down to meet the

---

[1] The Catechism tells us that the principal effects of baptism are "purification from sins and new birth in the Holy Spirit" (entry 1262), and all this is rooted in the fact that, according to St. Paul, "the believer enters through Baptism into communion with Christ's death, is buried with him, and rises with him" (*CCC* entry 1227; cf. Rom 6:3-4 and Col 2:12).

needs and overcome the miseries of His creatures. The Bible, the teachings of St. Thomas Aquinas, and Pope [St.] John Paul II all assure us that this is so. ...

Saint Thomas Aquinas defined mercy in general as "the compassion in our hearts for another person's misery, a compassion which drives us to do what we can to help him" (ST II-II.30.1). Divine Mercy, therefore, is the form that God's eternal love takes when He reaches out to us in our need and our brokenness. Whatever the nature of our need or our misery might be — sin, guilt, suffering, death — He is always ready to pour out His merciful, compassionate love for us, to help in time of need.[2]

By Divine Justice, on the other hand, we shall mean, first of all, what theologians traditionally called one form of God's "distributive justice" — in other words, *the attribute by which, in the end, He renders to each and all precisely what is their due for all the good and evil they have done.* With regard to rendering to unrepentant sinners what is their due, our Lord spoke of this clearly when He said in Matthew 16:27, "For the Son of Man is to come with his angels in the glory of his Father, and he will repay every man for what he has done." In Revelation 2:23 He says: "I am he who searches the mind and heart, and I will give to each of you as your works deserve." This is also what St. Paul taught in Romans 2:6-8: "For [God] will render to every man according to his works: to those who with patience in well-doing seek for glory and honor and immortality, he will give eternal life, but for those who are factious and do not obey the truth, but obey wickedness, there will be wrath and fury" (see also II Cor 5:10).

Holy Scripture and Sacred Tradition are emphatic: God is not

---

[2] Robert Stackpole, *Divine Mercy: A Guide from Genesis to Benedict XVI* (Stockbridge, Marian Press, revised edition, 2009), p. 19 and 26.

only a God of merciful love, He is also a God of judgment, including *the penal or retributive form of distributive justice*. In that sense, and in that sense alone, He is a God of "wrath" and "anger." In the Bible, these terms do not refer to emotions or temper-tantrums in God; they are simply metaphorical ways of speaking about His retributive justice. The trouble is that contemporary Catholic theology in general, and popular presentations of it in particular, tend to mute the uncomfortable truth about Divine Justice almost down to silence.

For some radical, dissident Catholic theologians, of course, there is no hell, there is no purgatory, nor does God ever chastise anyone in this life, nor is anything owed to God on the scales of justice because of our sins. We are not really guilty of serious sin anyway; just mentally and emotionally ill. In short, God comes across as really no more than a cosmic psychotherapist.

But it's not just the radicals who spread confusion about all this. In his otherwise outstanding book and DVD series, *Catholicism*, Bishop Robert Barron reassures us that even if there is a hell, we can "reasonably hope" that no one will ever end up there. Purgatory, he shows, is a place of spiritual healing — a painful healing process, to be sure — but not also a place of "temporal punishment" for half-repented sin (at least, he never explains in this book the judicial dimension of that purgatorial healing process). Moreover, Jesus may have done great things for us, but He did not need to die for our sins in the sense of making "satisfaction" for them to Divine Justice or "paying the penalty" for them on our behalf — in this book at least, Bishop Barron never mentions that aspect of the doctrine of the Cross at all.[3]

---

[3] More on Bishop Barron's contribution to these issues in the chapters to follow.

Why this shying away from the fullness of God's revelation here — even by many of the best Catholic writers today?

On the one hand, they shy away from speaking of the penal justice of God for very good pastoral and historical reasons. One could make the case that down through history, both Catholic and Protestant history, it was the merciful love of God that all too often was "muted" by theologians. They worked out grim scenarios of divine chastisements meted out by God in this present life, followed by purgatorial punishments or final condemnation in the life to come. This left far too many Christians in fear of God, but few who could truly love and trust Him. How can we forget that for more than 1,000 years, from the beginning of the Dark Ages until the end of the 19th century, most Christians, both east and west, were afraid to receive Holy Communion more than a handful of times per year, lest they receive unworthily and provoke Divine Judgment!

Given how deeply wounded many people are in our contemporary western world — wounded especially through family breakdown and dysfunction on an unprecedented scale — the first thing most people need to hear is that they have a Savior from all this misery, a Good Shepherd and Beloved Physician of the soul whom they can approach with trustful surrender of the heart, not a Judge who is standing over them, ready to issue a sentence of "guilty on all charges." Many people are so psychologically broken and confused these days that it's hard for them to sort out what they are really guilty of, and what they are not guilty of anyway. Many do not even understand the basics of the moral law. We are in a new era: not one that should lead us to deny the reality of sin and judgment, but one that should lead us to recognize that a lot of initial, remedial clarification needs to happen before most people can come to a true understanding of their sins, and an

7

authentic experience of divine forgiveness.

So I appreciate the historical and pastoral caution manifest, for example, in Bishop Barron's book. Nevertheless, Divine Justice and Final Judgment are revealed truths of the Christian faith, and again, as I shall explain later, we cannot fully appreciate the merciful love of God without a proper understanding of His penal, retributive justice too.

Talk of God's "retributive justice," of course, can make many people very anxious, and if not carefully expressed, it can lead to all kinds of misunderstanding. We all have hidden fears that God is not really merciful and compassionate; maybe God is a heartless Lawgiver after all, who one day will hunt us down and "get even" with us for every misstep we have ever taken. Let's be very clear right from the start, therefore, that this is not what we mean by God's "retributive" or "penal justice," which can never be separated from His merciful love. In my book *The Incarnation*, I defined God's penal justice like this:

> First, we need to define what we mean by "retributive punishment." With Steven L. Porter, I shall take this to mean, on a human level, "The forcible withdrawal of certain rights and/or privileges from a wrongdoer in response to the intentional misuse of those rights and/or privileges by the wrongdoer." By analogy, therefore, divine punishment for sin is the withdrawal of divine life from the unrepentant sinner: the loss of the life-giving Holy Spirit, resulting in temporal suffering and miseries of all kinds, and (in cases of unrepented mortal sin) eternal and irrevocable spiritual death. But this punishment does not take the form of a divine act additional to the sin itself. Rather, *by God's design, sin brings about its own punishment.* In other words, divine, retributive punishment for sin is an expression of God's *permissive will*: he permits us to misuse our free-will, if we so choose, and in accord with his

justice allows the stubbornly impenitent to experience the inevitable consequences of their unrepented sins — what sin by its very nature brings: the obstruction, or even eviction (so to speak) of the life-giving Holy Spirit from the soul, resulting in both increased temporal sufferings, and ultimately eternal loss. And it is just and right that God permits this. In other words, as an expression of his attribute of distributive justice by which he renders to each person what is their due, God has made the world and human life in such a way that ultimately, both in this life and the next, justice is done in the lives of those who refuse to repent for their wickedness, and who reject his mercy.[4]

The *Catechism of the Catholic Church* sums it up for us in entry 1864:

> There are no limits to the mercy of God, but anyone who deliberately refuses to accept his mercy by repenting, rejects the forgiveness of his sins and the salvation offered by the Holy Spirit.

One of the underlying problems in the Church today, it seems to me, is that many Catholics have bought into the modern view that God's attributes of justice and mercy are really incompatible opposites, alternative and mutually exclusive ways in which He might relate to His creatures, whereas classical Christian teaching saw them as united in the infinite mystery of God's own nature. Somehow, God's justice is always exercised with mercy, and His mercy is never unjust.

Pope Benedict XVI echoed the classical Christian understanding of God when he said in 2011:

---

[4] Robert Stackpole, *The Incarnation: Rediscovering Kenotic Christology* (Chilliwack, BC: The Chartwell Press, 2019), p. 454.

For us, "just" means "what is due to the other," while "merciful" is what is given out of kindness. One seems to exclude the other. Yet for God it is not like this: justice and charity *coincide* in him; there is no just action that is not also an act of mercy and pardon, and at the same time, there is no merciful action that is not perfectly just.[5]

Pope Benedict was not trying to say, however, that Divine Mercy and Divine Justice are "equal" in priority or importance to God. In the book of James, chapter two, verse 13, the apostle tells us that as a general principle, God's "mercy triumphs over justice." Moreover, our Lord told St. Faustina that she should "Proclaim that mercy is the greatest attribute of God. All the works of My hands are crowned with mercy" (*Diary*, entry 300), a teaching reiterated a half-century later by Pope St. John Paul II in his encyclical letter *Dives in Misericordia* (*Rich in Mercy*, section 13): "The Bible, Tradition, and the whole faith life of the People of God provide unique proof ... that mercy is the greatest of the attributes and perfections of God."

In his *Summa Theologiae*, St. Thomas Aquinas taught that "The work of Divine Justice always presupposes the work of mercy and is based upon it" (*ST* I. 21. 4). In other words, as we shall see in this book, God fulfills His merciful plan for the human race not by ignoring or cancelling the requirements of His justice, but by fulfilling them — and going way beyond them — always putting His justice at the service of His merciful love for us.

---

[5] Pope Benedict XVI, Address at his Pastoral Visit to Rebibbia District Prison in Rome, Sunday, December 18, 2011, accessed online at http://w2.vatican.va/content/benedict-xvi/en/speeches/2011/december/ documents/hf_ben-xvi_spe_20111218_rebibbia.html

In fact, some of the greatest saints and theologians in Catholic history sought to find ways to fuse together in a single vision God's justice and His mercy. For instance, St. Therese of Lisieux, "The Little Flower," found comfort and consolation when it dawned on her that God's justice could be seen in the light of His mercy:

> I understand ... that all souls cannot be the same, that it is necessary there be different types in order to honor each of God's perfections in a particular way. To me He has granted His *infinite mercy*, and *through it* I contemplate and adore the other divine perfections! All of these perfections appear to be resplendent with *love*, even His justice (and perhaps this even more so than others) seems to me clothed in love. What a sweet joy it is to think that God is Just, i.e., that He takes into account our weakness, that He is perfectly aware of our fragile nature. What should I fear then? Ah! must not the infinitely just God, who deigns to pardon the faults of the prodigal son with so much kindness, be just also toward me, who "am with Him always? (Lk 15:31)[6]

To be sure, this is a mystery — the absolute inseparability of Divine Mercy and Divine Justice — that we can never completely fathom with our limited minds. As I explained in *Divine Mercy: A Guide*, however, even in this life

> we can begin to see that God's justice — His occasional chastisements of us in this life, and His purgatorial punishments of us in the next — are also, at one and the

---

[6] Saint Therese of Lisieux, *Story of a Soul: The Autobiography of St. Therese of Lisieux* (Washington, DC: Institute of Carmelite Studies, third edition, 1996), p. 180.

same time, expressions of His mercy toward us. If He sometimes chastises us by permitting us to suffer, it is only to "wake us up" and summon us back to repentance and faith ("Those whom the Lord loves, He chastises" [Heb 12:6]), and Purgatory is not only a place of temporal punishment for half-repented sin; it is also, at the same time, a "purging" that mercifully sanctifies and heals the soul (see *Catechism*, 1030).

More difficult to fathom is how the final damnation of a soul is also, in another way, God's final act of mercy toward that soul. ... And yet we can know right from the start that it must be so: [the Catholic philosophical tradition] shows us that God's nature is absolutely simple and indivisible, so that His justice must always be an expression of His mercy. [In fact] the simplicity and indivisibility of the divine nature was a truth solemnly defined at the First Vatican Council, *Dogmatic Constitution on the Catholic Faith*, Chapter One. Moreover, the Psalms clearly state that God's mercy is over all His works (see Ps 145:9).[7]

Most of all, as we shall see, the Cross of Jesus supremely expresses both the merciful love and the penal justice of God, at one and the same time. As a result of our sins, our moral debt to Divine Justice was so vast that only the God of Mercy, dwelling among us as a fully human being, as Jesus Christ, could atone for our sins, and clear that debt for us.

---

[7] Stackpole, *Divine Mercy: A Guide from Genesis to Benedict XVI*, p. 96. This also means that God is never purely "vengeful" or "vindictive": pejorative words that refer to the pursuit of retributive justice apart from any connection with mercy and compassion. God's retributive justice, however, can never be separated from His mercy. All of the perfections of God — such as His love, justice, power and wisdom — are eternally inseparable in the divine nature.

Unfortunately, it's not just the retributive, penal justice of God that is often overlooked by Catholics today. Devotees of the Divine Mercy often forget that God's merciful love demands that we seek "social justice" as well. Social justice involves making sure that each person receives what they have a right to expect from the social order. Proclaiming Divine Mercy without seeking social justice for all, as much as we can, is a scandalous sin of omission.

Consider what the Book of Isaiah in the Old Testament teaches us. On the one hand, the prophet repeatedly states that "justice," "holiness" and "righteousness" are essential characteristics of God. Isaiah's favorite term for the Lord, in fact, was "the Holy One of Israel," and he does not mince words on this aspect of the divine nature: "The Lord of hosts is exalted in justice, and the Holy God shows himself holy in righteousness" (Is 5:16). On the other hand, by these terms and phrases it's pretty clear that Isaiah did not mean only "penal" or "retributive" justice. Rather, for Isaiah *God's justice is his commitment to set things right in his world in every respect* — and not just by holding accountable unrepentant evildoers. For example, His justice also impels him to seek fairness and relief for the poor; "Happy is he whose help is the God of Jacob, whose hope is in the Lord his God ... who executes justice for the oppressed; who gives food to the hungry" (Ps 146: 5-7). And what could be more clear and challenging than Isaiah's call to social justice in chapter 58:

> Is this not the fast that I choose: to loose the bonds of wickedness, to undo the thongs of the yoke, to let the oppressed go free, and to break every yoke? Is it not to share your bread with the hungry, and bring the homeless poor into your house; when you see the naked to cover him, and not to hide yourself from your own flesh? Then shall your light break forth like the dawn, and your healing

shall spring up speedily; your righteousness shall go before you, the glory of the Lord shall be your rear guard. Then you shall call, and the Lord will answer; you shall cry, and he will say, Here I am. (Is 58: 6-9)

This aspect of Divine Justice, too, we shall explore in the chapters to come.

In short, in this book I hope to show how important it is to our Catholic faith — and especially to the Divine Mercy message and devotion — to believe that God is always perfectly just and perfectly merciful in all that He does for us, and all that He asks of us. Unless we really understand this, our devotion to the Divine Mercy will become merely slushy and sentimental, rather than the life-changing, world-transforming expression of the gospel that our Lord intended it to be.

Chapter Two
The Cross and the Confessional:
Where Mercy and Justice Meet

None of us like to think of God as the great Policeman or the great Bookkeeper in the sky, the One who keeps a strict account of all of our sins. But that is how some people think of God today — and why they try not to, and try to avoid him as much as possible. To them, the Cross of Jesus atop the spire of their local church is not a sign of God's merciful love for us, but a sign that makes them feel guilty, with nowhere to turn. They think to themselves: "A God who takes sin that seriously, even making His Son bear the penalty for all our sins, is not liable to have much mercy on a hardened sinner like me, carrying so much baggage from the past."

At the same time, many Catholics today go to the opposite extreme. They object to the Church's traditional teaching about the Cross. They contend that this teaching makes it appear as if God is only interested in balancing a ledger book in Heaven of our merits and demerits, in other words, that all He cares about is the "justice" side of things: punishing the unrepentant, and clearing the moral debts of the penitent through the death of His Son. "None of that makes sense if we really believe in a God of *love*," they say. "The *only* thing God *really* cares about is reestablishing a loving personal relationship with His lost children, like the father of the prodigal son in Jesus' parable."[1] So, in this day and age we

---

[1] Of course, this argument presupposes that the Parable of the Prodigal Son was meant by our Lord to be a complete exposition of *every* aspect of God's redeeming love and redeeming work, rather than as vivid portrayal of one (albeit the most important) aspect: divine compassion for sinners.

need to "reinterpret" the doctrine of the Atonement in purely personal, relational terms, these Catholics say, rather than repeat the old harsh, judicial, "transactional" theories involving guilt and punishment. Thus, when we say the prayers called "The Chaplet of Divine Mercy," which speak of offering up "the Body and Blood, soul and divinity of Jesus Christ in atonement for our sins," we wrongly continue the old inadequate, judicial understanding of Jesus Christ's work of reconciliation. We should focus instead on the Cross as a sign of God's patient, forbearing, and unconditional love for us all.

These two perspectives on the Cross may seem to be "polar opposites;" but, as a matter of fact, they share something very important in common: they are both quite wrong.

Holy Scripture and the Magisterium on the Saving Work of Jesus on The Cross

There is no question that sometimes the Catholic faith has been presented in a misleading way. As we discussed in the first chapter of this book, Jesus Christ's saving work must be an expression both of God's love *and* His justice: not of His justice alone, or of His love alone. We must not set up in our minds here what philosophers call a "false dichotomy" (A false dichotomy occurs when we claim that there's an opposition between two statements or two ideas that, on closer examination, are not really opposed to each other after all). As we shall see, the gospel message of Divine Mercy does not contradict the holiness or the justice of God.

The simple fact is that both Scripture and Catholic tradition often use transactional and judicial — and even commercial

— language to describe aspects of what Jesus Christ has done for us to save us from the penalty and power of sin. And this is not seen in isolation from God's personal love for us at all. For example, in Mark 10:45, Jesus tells His disciples, "For the Son of Man also came not to be served, but to serve, and to give His life as a ransom for many." A "ransom," in the original Greek of Saint Mark's gospel, was a merciful, financial transaction: making a payment that sets a slave free. In ancient Israel, people usually became slaves as a social penalty, because they could not pay their debts — so a "ransom" payment cleared their debts in order to liberate them.[2] Indeed, Saint Paul states repeatedly that we are all "bought with a price" (1 Cor 6:20). The New Testament uses judicial

---

[2] In his book *Salvation: What Every Catholic Should Know* (San Francisco and Greenwood Village, CO: Ignatius Press and the Augustine Institute, 2019), p. 37-52, Michael Patrick Barber devotes most of one chapter to a discussion of the biblical understanding of sin and atonement. In the Old Testament, sin was considered as a kind of "debt" to God, and God himself was Israel's redeemer who cleared that debt for them, in various ways. The idea of sin as a moral debt to God that needed to be paid so that we could be set free from the guilt and punishment of our sins is carried over into the New Testament:

> In Colossians we read that Jesus's death dissolves the "debt" humanity owed to God: "[God] has forgiven all our trespasses, by *cancelling the record of debt* that stood against us with its legal demands. This he set aside, nailing it to the cross" (Colossians 2:13-14).

> Sin is a debt. Christ pays the price of "redemption" to save us from it by giving his very self on our behalf. As Jesus says in the Gospels ... he came to "give his life as a ransom for many" (Matthew 20:28; Mark 10:45; cf. also Ephesians 1:7; I Peter 1: 18-19). (Barber, p. 46).

language when Saint Paul tells us, "Christ redeemed us from the curse of the law by becoming a curse for us," (Gal 3:13), and Saint Paul refers in the same passage to the Old Testament, which states that anyone who is executed on a tree is cursed by God (cf. Dt 21:23).

In what way did Christ bear a divine "curse" for us? The Old Testament passage that the early Christians saw as a special clue to Christ's saving work (which is why it is enshrined in our Good Friday Liturgy) is the prophecy about the suffering Servant of the Lord who bears the penalty that we deserve for our sins. This is found especially in Isaiah, Chapter 53, verse 5:

> But He was wounded for our transgressions. He was bruised for our iniquities, upon Him was the chastisement that made us whole, and with His stripes we are healed. All we, like sheep, have gone astray, we have turned everyone to his own way, and the Lord has laid on Him the iniquity of us all.

Saint John's first epistle uses sacrificial language to make much the same point: "In this is love, not that we love God but that He loved us and sent His Son to be the expiation [or propitiation][3] for our sins" (1 Jn 4:10). Similarly, according to the Book of Hebrews, chapters 8 through 10, the sacrificial offering and shedding of Christ's blood on the Cross wins something for us that the animal sacrifices in the Jewish temple could never really obtain: the forgiveness of our sins.

In the Gospels we also see Jesus offered a "cup" to drink by his heavenly Father in the Garden of Gethsemane. It is commonly assumed that this "cup" was simply the cup of his

---

[3] Either way this passage is translated from the Greek, the word refers to a sacrificial offering that, in effect, turns away the wrath of God.

betrayal, and the excruciating sufferings he would have to undergo in his agony and passion. But a closer look at the biblical metaphor of the "cup" that the Lord sometimes gives people to drink shows that its roots go much deeper. No doubt the "cup" has several layers of meaning, but one layer surely refers to the "cup" of divine "wrath" for sin (that is, divine retributive justice) — a "cup" mentioned with this same connotation at least 10 times in Holy Scripture.[4] Jesus knew very well what he was getting into by drinking that cup to the dregs on the Cross; he was offering himself as a special kind of sacrifice: a sin-bearing sacrifice for lost and broken humanity.

In short, God loved us so much that God Himself, in the person of His Son, bore the burden and penalty of our sins on the Cross so that we might be offered forgiveness on a just basis, and so that the sanctifying grace of God might be poured out upon us. Clearly in doing all this for us, the divine Son of God, Jesus Christ, manifested both His perfect justice, and His perfect love, at one at the same time. In other words, He fulfilled the demands of His justice out of His infinite, merciful love for us. Pope St. John Paul II taught us this same truth in his encyclical *"Dives In Misericordia"* (*Rich in Mercy* section 7):

> In the Passion and Death of Christ, in the fact that the Father did not spare His own Son, but for our own sake made Him sin, absolute justice is expressed, for Christ undergoes the Passion and Cross because of the sins of humanity. This constitutes even a superabundance of justice, for the sins of Man are compensated for by the sacrifice of the Man-God. Nevertheless, this justice,

---

[4] See Job 21:20; Ezek 23:32-34; Is 51:17-22; Ps 75:8; Jer 25:15-29; Hab 2:16 and 49:12; also Rev 14:10, 16:1ff, and 18:6.

which is properly justice to God's measure, springs completely from love, from the love of the Father and the Son, and completely, bears fruit in love. Precisely for this reason the divine justice revealed in the cross of Christ is "to God's measure," because it springs from love and is accomplished in love, producing fruits of salvation.

In a similar way, the *Catechism* describes this aspect of Christ's saving work as, in part, a judicial accomplishment, that is, He takes away the penalty for our sin by substituting Himself for us on the Cross (entry 615):

> By His obedience unto death, Jesus accomplished the substitution of the suffering Servant, who 'makes an *offering for sin*' when 'He bore the sin of many,' and who 'shall make many to be accounted righteous,' for 'He shall bear their iniquities.' Jesus atoned for our faults, and made satisfaction for our sins to the Father.

To sum up: both Scripture and the Church's *magisterium* teach us that one very important aspect of Jesus Christ's saving work was in fact, transactional. To be sure, *the mystery of redemption is multi-dimensional*, and cannot be completely expressed by one particular theory, or completely captured in one set of metaphors. Nevertheless, one of its dimensions is clearly transactional: our Lord made up for our sins by dying for us on the Cross. Indeed He *more than made up* for our sins. As St. John Paul II put it, His offering before God's justice was of such great value that it was a "superabundant" sacrifice for sin. In other words, He not only cleared away our debt to Divine Justice, He also merited for us all the graces that we need for the sanctification of our hearts, and the gift of eternal life.

Perhaps now we can see why it's unfair to say that Catholic teaching about Christ's saving work, expressed in the wording of the Chaplet as well as in the *Catechism*, is *merely* transactional, as if by that we meant, "merely impersonal in some way", or "merely about God's justice and not also about His personal love for us". In His infinite Holiness, God cannot just forget about our mortal sins, and pretend they are unimportant — letting bygones be bygones, so to speak. That would trivialize them, and imply that He does not take our sins very seriously. The *Catechism* tells us that sin is a destructive force that leaves behind all kinds of harm in its wake: it violates human dignity (entries 1700 and 1714), separates people from each other (845), wounds the unity and mission of the Church (817 and 953), and robs humanity of its resemblance to God (705). Most importantly, sin violates our proper, personal relationship with God himself, our heavenly Father.

Even in human relationships, we see that just brushing aside grievous wrongdoing is almost never the path to true reconciliation. When someone seriously wrongs or injures you, don't they *owe you* something before forgiveness can be fully granted and friendship fully restored? A sincere apology, at least? And in more extreme cases, some kind of compensatory restitution or reparation? Perhaps they need to pay a debt to society as well, by serving time in prison. In any case, a personal relationship or friendship cannot be fully restored without that real moral debt somehow being acknowledged and made up.[5]

---

[5] In my book *the Incarnation*, p. 413-414, I explored the charge that proper claims for the satisfaction of penal justice amount to the imposition of an abstract and extrinsic standard upon personal relationships. On the contrary, they flow from the very mystery of personal relationship itself. For example, in commenting on the thought of Richard Swinburne on this subject, I explained:

No wrong that we can commit is more grievous than when we seriously betray or let down someone who loved and trusted us. *Human sin, in fact, is a betrayal of our heavenly Father's infinite love for us.* Out of His infinite love He created us, gave us the gift of life, gave us each other and all of creation to care for, and offered us the possibility of eternal life with Him in Heaven. By our sins, however, we betray that free gift of love — *and that surely leaves us in a state of tremendous moral debt to God.* We really owe Him something that we can never repay: namely a life of faithful service of the good purposes for which He made us. Having misspent our past, we have nothing "extra" to offer to God to make up for it now. But Jesus Christ, the divine Son, made up for our sins on our

---

In an essay first published in 1988, "The Christian Scheme of Salvation," Richard Swinburne developed a Sacrificial-Satisfaction theory based on the premise that a righteous God cannot fully forgive us for our sins unless we have made an adequate atonement for them. For God to do otherwise, for him simply to overlook our past sins, requiring nothing of us, would trivialise our past wrong-doing, and imply that he does not take sin or personal relations very seriously.

It would be a mistake to interpret Swinburne as insisting here on an abstract standard of justice "extrinsic" to our personal relationship with God. Rather, the strength of his theory is his insight that real personal relationships include the need for just compensation to be offered when wrongs have been committed. Only personal beings among God's creatures can practice this virtue of justice: it is only human beings who can say things like "that's not fair," or "I owe you an apology" or "he paid his debt to society"— expressive of what we all believe is an essential aspect of personal and social relationships. Presumably, our relationship with God has this dimension as well, who alone possesses the attribute of justice (i.e., the commitment to render to each person what is due to them) in an infinitely perfect way.

behalf, by His obedient life and His death on the Cross. As I have written elsewhere: "He made up for our misspent past, and bore the penalty we deserve. He also merited for us all the sanctifying graces that can heal us and set us free from sin's power. That's not just some cold, impersonal, judicial transaction. It's a wonderful gift of His mercy that sets us free from the penalty and power of sin," if only we will receive that gift by opening our hearts to Jesus more and more by true repentance and faith.[6] Saint Paul put it best: "While we were yet helpless, at the right time Christ died for the ungodly. Why, one will hardly die for a righteous man — though perhaps for a good man, one will dare even to die. But God shows His love for us in that while we were yet sinners Christ died for us" (Rom 5: 6-8).

Missing in Action: The Penal Dimension of Christ's Saving Work in Contemporary Catholic Thought

Now I am going to cause some trouble. I am going to criticize the writings of several of the best Catholic theologians of our time. I am going to show that (no doubt, inadvertently) they have sometimes exchanged the clear and life-transforming gospel of the saving death of Jesus Christ for a vague, metaphorical fog.

For example, let's look first at an excellent book (one that we mentioned before) titled *Catholicism* by Bishop Robert Barron. Here is what Bishop Barron has to say in that book about what Jesus accomplished for us by His Passion and Death:

> Jesus was met by betrayal, denial, institutional corruption, violence, stupidity, deep injustice, and incomparable cruelty, but he did not respond in kind. Rather, like the

---

[6] Ibid., p. 546-547.

scapegoat, upon whom all the sins of Israel were symbolically placed on the Day of Atonement, Jesus took upon himself the sins of the world. As he hung from the cross, he became sin, as Saint Paul would later put it, and bearing the full weight of that disorder he said, "Father forgive them, they know not what they do" (Luke 23:34). Jesus on the cross drowned all the sins of the world in the infinite ocean of the divine mercy, and that is how he fought. We can see here how important it is to affirm the divinity of Jesus, for if he were only a human being, his death on the cross would be, at best, an inspiring example of dedication and courage. But as the Son of God, Jesus died a death that transfigured the world. The theological tradition has said that God the Father was pleased with the sacrifice of his Son, but we should never interpret this along sadistic lines as though the Father needed to see the suffering of his Son in order to assuage his infinite anger. The Father loved the willingness of the Son to go to the very limits of God-forsakenness — all the way to the bottom of sin — in order to manifest the divine mercy. The Father loved the courage of his Son, the non-violent warrior.[7]

In short, according to Bishop Barron, Jesus somehow "drowned all the sins of the world in the infinite ocean of divine mercy" by suffering from them non-violently, and this death "transfigured the world" because He was willing to go to the very "bottom" of the experience of God-forsakenness in order "to manifest divine mercy." OK, but how does that work? How does the divine Son of God's patient, non-retaliatory suffering from the cruelty and injustices inflicted on Him long ago actually accomplish all that? We are not told — at least, not with any clarity. Bishop Barron begins to unfold

[7] Robert Barron, *Catholicism* (New York: Image Books, 2011), p. 31.

the mystery when he writes: "Like the scapegoat, upon whom all the sins of Israel were symbolically placed on the Day of Atonement, Jesus took upon himself the sins of the world." But what this might mean is never explained.

The Old Testament reveals much about God's patience and long-suffering — so after reading Bishop Barron's account of Christ's saving work on the Cross, we need to ask: What does Christ on the Cross "manifest" to us about Divine Mercy that God's patience and long-suffering with His wayward People Israel did not already show? Bishop Barron says that Jesus Christ, as the divine Son incarnate, suffers all this evil and injustice in person for us, in the flesh — granted, *but why did He need to do that? What did His suffering in the flesh actually accomplish for us,* beyond reiterating for us, in a more vivid way, what the Jews already knew: that the Lord is "gracious and merciful, long-suffering and abounding in steadfast love" (Ps 103)?

Bishop Barron further tells us that if God's "anger" (presumably His retributive justice?) needed to be "assuaged" in some way, then that would be "sadistic." So, divine retributive justice for unrepented mortal sin is the same as sadism?

We have been dropped into a metaphorical soup here, and while all the ingredients may be there, the actual recipe of Christ's redeeming work is not clearly explained to the reader.

Now, metaphors in theology are very important. They help us to begin to grasp the inexpressible mystery of the depths of God's love for us in ways that mere scientific, philosophical or abstract terminology can never do on its own. Still, metaphors are put to best use when they deepen and amplify clear thinking about the doctrines of the faith — not when they replace it! Where is the dimension of the classical gospel message here in Bishop Barron's teachings on the Cross that Jesus Christ died to fulfill the demands of Divine Justice as well as to manifest His Divine Love for us? Where is the traditional Catholic doctrine that God the Son manifested Divine Mercy on the Cross precisely by paying the penalty for us — or making "satisfaction" to Divine Justice — in our place and for our sake?[8]

I wish that this oversight in Bishop Barron's book was merely an isolated incident in Catholic theology today, but unfortunately it is not.

In his book *Jesus the Christ*, Fr. Thomas Weinandy, OFM Cap., tells us that it was not the Father's "righteous anger" that required the death of Jesus on the Cross:

> Jesus' sacrifice must not be seen as placating an angry God, as if he were an offended person who demanded in justice to be propitiated and appeased. It is sin itself, in conformity with the justice of God, that has justly imposed upon humankind a debt, and it is this debt that is expiated through the death of Jesus.[9]

To be sure, if we take words such as "angry," "offended," "placating" and "appeased" as describing emotional states in God, or pure vindictiveness (that is, a desire for retributive justice *apart from* love and compassion), then it would be a gross caricature of the gospel to say that the Father's "righteous anger" needed to be cooled off somehow by the death of Jesus before He could forgive us! But that is not

---

[8] See Appendix B for further discussion of this point.
[9] Thomas Weinandy, OFM Cap., *Jesus the Christ* (Huntington, IN : Our Sunday Visitor, 2003), p. 111 and 115.

26

what the classical doctrine of the Cross said. As previously discussed, words such as "wrath" and "anger" when applied to God are merely metaphors for His distributive, penal justice. Furthermore, Jesus cannot exactly "appease" an "angry God" because He is Himself God incarnate: as divine Son and Judge of the world, He is every bit as committed to fulfilling the demands of Divine Justice as His heavenly Father. Finally, Fr. Weinandy seems to have stopped just a half-step short of expressing the full implications of his own teaching here. If "sin itself, in conformity with the justice of God, has justly imposed upon humankind a debt" that must be "expiated", then it must be equally true to say that we are in moral debt to Divine Justice from our sins, and that we ought to offer God some kind of reparation or compensation to clear that debt. One dimension of the gospel message has always been that God Himself, in the person of His Son, out of His merciful love for us, paid that debt for us on the Cross. We sing this at every Easter in the Easter *Exultet*:

> It is truly right and good, always and everywhere, with our whole heart and mind and voice, to praise you the invisible, almighty and eternal God, and your only begotten Son, Jesus Christ our Lord; for he is the true Paschal Lamb, who *at the feast of the Passover paid for us the debt of Adam's sin, and by his blood delivered your faithful people.*

Sadly, this gospel of the Cross seems to get lost in the fog even more in Pope Benedict XVI's great book, *Jesus of Nazareth: Volume Two*. The Pope stated in the "Introduction" that his book was merely intended to be a scholarly exploration, and not an exercise of his papal magisterium, much less a definitive statement of Catholic doctrine. So, in offering a critique of what he wrote about the Cross in that book, I am in no way being disobedient to papal teaching authority. In any case, regarding the Cross Pope Benedict wrote:

In Jesus' Passion, all the filth of the world touches the infinitely pure one, the soul of Jesus Christ, and hence, the Son of God himself. While it is usually the case that anything unclean touching something clean renders it unclean, here it is the other way around: when the world, with all the injustice and cruelty that makes it unclean, comes into contact with the infinitely pure one — then he, the pure one, is the stronger. Through this contact, the filth of the world is truly absorbed, wiped out and transformed in the pain of infinite love. Because infinite good is now at hand in the man Jesus, the counterweight to all wickedness is present and active within world history, and the good is always infinitely greater than the mass of evil, however terrible it may be.

If we reflect more deeply on this insight, we find the answer to an objection that is often raised against the idea of atonement. Again and again, people say: It must be a cruel God who demands infinite atonement. Is this not a notion unworthy of God? Must we not give up the idea of atonement in order to maintain the purity of our image of God? In the [New Testament] use of the term *hilasterion* [an expiatory or propitiatory offering] with reference to Jesus, it becomes evident that the real forgiveness accomplished on the Cross functions in exactly the opposite direction. The reality of evil and injustice that disfigures the world and at the same time distorts the image of God — this reality exists through our sin. It cannot simply be ignored; it must be addressed. But here it is not a case of a cruel God demanding the infinite. It is exactly the opposite: God himself becomes the locus of reconciliation, and in the person of his Son taking the suffering upon himself grants his infinite purity to the world. God himself "drinks the cup" of every horror to the dregs and thereby restores justice through the greatness of his love, which through suffering transforms the darkness.[10]

As with Bishop Barron and Fr. Weinandy, the problem here is not so much with what Pope Benedict says about the Cross, but with what he does not say. He seems to push aside any idea that anything infinite — or at any rate any debt unpayable by us — is owed to God's justice because of our sins. At the end of the passage Pope Benedict writes vaguely that Christ "restores justice through the greatness of his love," but according to Pope Benedict (at least in the way he expresses the mystery of redemption in this particular book), that evidently does not mean that Christ pays the penalty for our sins, or offers "satisfaction" to Divine Justice because of our sins. So we can only turn to the rest of the passage to find out what Pope Benedict really does mean here.

We are told that Christ on the Cross becomes the "locus" (or the "place") of reconciliation between God and man, by "granting his infinite purity to the world" and "drinking to the dregs every horror," and thereby somehow through His suffering "transforming the darkness." No doubt all these metaphors are true in some sense — but in what sense? A person's unjust suffering — even the deepest possible unjust sufferings undergone by a divine person in human flesh — would still not seem to do much to overcome evil in the world, other than to display God's patient, forbearing nature. Where in all this is the full, classical teaching of the saints and of the Council of Trent that "Jesus Christ, by His most Holy Passion on the Cross, offered satisfaction for us to God the Father" — that is, the satisfaction both of His Father's merciful love and of His retributive justice?

---

[10] Pope Benedict XVI, *Jesus of Nazareth: Part Two* (San Francisco: Ignatius Press, 2011) p. 231-232.

I have two reasons for being especially concerned about all this.

First, if even the best Catholic theologians of our time cannot clearly express the Gospel of the Cross, then the New Evangelization that the popes have been calling for over the past few decades is not going to succeed. To "evangelize" obviously includes spreading the "Good News" about what Jesus Christ has done for us. But if we cannot clearly state that Good News, then we cannot effectively share it.[11]

The second reason is more embarrassing to me personally. I am afraid I helped to spread some of this fog of confusion myself ....

Time to eat some humble pie.

---

[11] Just to clarify: I am not claiming here that Bishop Barron, Fr. Weinandy, and Pope Benedict inadequately express the Gospel of the Cross *throughout their writings*: I am only referring to what I perceive to be the shortcomings of these particular books that I have cited, popular books that have been widely disseminated to the Catholic public. I contend that if you did not know the contours of the traditional Gospel of the Cross beforehand, you would find it very difficult to make it out from these three books. It may be that elsewhere, however, in other, more scholarly books, the authors have expressed themselves on this mystery of the faith more clearly. Moreover, several saints of the Church, and several recent Catholic theologians have taken pains to defend the notion of Christ's death as a penal substitution or satisfaction of Divine Justice. The list here would include St. Alphonsus De Liguori, a Doctor of the Church, and the Ven. Fulton J. Sheen, and among recent theologians Hans Urs Von Balthasar, Cardinal Walter Kasper, and Fr. Raniero Cantalamessa, OFM Cap. For an in-depth discussion of this theological issue, see my book *The Incarnation: Rediscovering Kenotic Christology*, p. 434-493.

In my first book, *Jesus, Mercy Incarnate,* I had this to say about the Passion and Death of our Savior:

> The problem with the [substitutionary] point of view is that even if God wanted to take proper retribution for our sins upon Himself, justice would not be served. Strict justice does not say "a sin has been committed — *someone* must suffer for it," but "a sin has been committed — *the guilty party* must suffer for it" (cf. Ez 18: 1-4). Thus, the innocent divine Son could not justly bear the retribution we deserve. As one theologian wrote: "Justice can never be served by punishing the innocent. ... If [the Son of] God then deliberately takes on Himself the suffering which is my due for the evil I have done, He is not satisfying Justice; He is perverting it. His conduct may be considered admirable from a different point of view, but not from that of Justice."[12]

It is clear to me now that this argument does not hold water. Here's why: We know very well that a mere human person cannot justly be punished in place of, and for the crimes of, another. No one can justly assume the punishment due to another, even if he volunteers to do so (except under certain limited and exceptional circumstances).[13] But Jesus Christ was

---

[12] Robert Stackpole, *Jesus, Mercy Incarnate* (Stockbridge, MA: Marian Press, 2000), p. 44-45.

[13] Two exceptions spring to mind. (1) We normally do not find it unjust for one person to help another pay off his *financial* debts or fines. Voluntary financial substitutionary debt repayment is usually considered acceptable, and even commendable (as long as the debtor is truly contrite, and truly unable to repay his debts himself). (2) In the Church, the Mystical Body of Christ, we are so deeply bonded together by the Holy Spirit as members one of another (I Cor 12:12-26), that it seems to be possible for one member voluntarily to assume the *temporal* punishment due to the sins of

31

not a mere human person; He *was and is the divine Son of God in human form* — and we do not know that it is unjust for *Him* to take upon Himself the burden and penalty of our sins. After all, no one else in the whole universe stands in the same relationship to us as He does, for He alone is our Creator and our Judge.

Imagine a judge in a court of law who pronounces a verdict of "guilty as charged," and justly sentences the accused and his family to pay massive reparations for their crimes — reparation payments so huge that the family will have to pay off the debt for the rest of their lives. Then imagine the same judge, out of mercy and compassion for that family, coming down from the bench and offering to "foot the bill" to clear those payments, even at terrible cost to himself. Here we have an analogy (albeit an imperfect one, as all analogies for divine mysteries must be) of what our Creator, Judge and Savior,

---

another (but not the *eternal* punishment for sin; for an explanation of these two kinds of punishment, see Catechism, entry 1472, and the next chapter of this book). They can do so by performing works of piety, penances and mortifications on their behalf. But of course, the sinner's debt of temporal punishment is not thereby *automatically* cleared. What actually happens in this kind of "transaction" within the Body of Christ is that the one member, by his works of penance in a state of grace, simply merits the graces of deeper repentance and conversion for another — but only if that other person then freely cooperates with those graces, and thereby actually attains that spiritual state of deeper repentance and conversion, can the temporal punishment due to his sins be remitted. To be sure, a soul in Purgatory would certainly cooperate with those special, additional graces, obtained on their behalf, and in that sense works of piety, or indulgences offered up on the behalf of these Holy Souls unfailingly obtains the remission of some or all of their temporal punishment due to sin. For a more complete explanation of all this, see Chapter Three of this book.

Jesus Christ, has done for us.

In his work "Reflections and Affections on the Passion of Jesus Christ," St. Alphonsus Liguori (1696-1787), Doctor of the Church and founder of the Congregation of the Most Holy Redeemer, powerfully expressed this doctrine of Christ's saving work on the Cross. He wrote:

> The Son of God, the Lord of the universe, seeing that man was condemned to eternal death in punishment of his sins, chose to take upon himself human flesh, and thus to pay by his death the penalty due to man. ... "But how is this?" continues St. Augustine. How is it possible, O Saviour of the world, that Thy love has arrived at such a height that when I had committed the crime, Thou shouldst have to pay the penalty? "Whither has Thy love reached? I have sinned; Thou art punished." ...
>
> Our loving Redeemer, having come into the world for no other end but that of saving sinners, and beholding the sentence of condemnation already recorded against us for our sins, what was it that he did? He, by his own death paid the penalty that was due to ourselves; and with his own blood cancelling the sentence of condemnation, in order that divine justice might no more seek from us the satisfaction due, he nailed it to the same cross whereon he died (Col 2:14).[14]

The Ven. Archbishop Fulton J. Sheen (1895-1979) probed this mystery in-depth, explaining that when Christ on the Cross offered up his cry of agony and desolation, "My God, My God, why have you forsaken me?" at that very moment he

---

[14] Saint Alphonsus De Liguori, *The Passion and Death of Jesus Christ* (Brooklyn: Redemptorist Fathers, 1927), p. 25, and 130.

experienced in his sacred humanity something analogous to the guilt and alienation of every lost soul, and thereby bore the eternal punishment for all human sin:

> Sinners can show a love for one another by taking the punishment which another deserves. But our Blessed Lord was not only taking the punishment but also taking the guilt as if it were His own ....

> In taking upon Himself the sins of the world [Jesus Christ] willed a kind of withdrawal of His Father's face and all Divine consolation.... This particular moment He willed to take upon Himself that principal effect of sin which was abandonment.

> Man rejected God; so now He willed to feel that rejection. Man turned away from God; now He, Who was God united personally with a human nature, willed to feel in that human nature that awful wrench as if He Himself were guilty .... In that cry [of dereliction on the Cross] were all the sentiments in human hearts expressive of a Divine nostalgia: the loneliness of the atheist, the skeptic, the pessimist, the sinners who hate themselves for hating virtue, and of all those who have no love above the flesh; for to be without love is hell. It was, therefore, the moment when leaning on nails He stood at the brink of hell in the name of all sinners. As He entered upon the extreme penalty of sin, which is separation from God, it was fitting that His eyes be filled with darkness and His soul with loneliness. ...

> Christ's cry was of abandonment which He felt standing in a sinner's place, but it was not of despair. The soul that despairs never cries to God .... The emptiness of humanity through sin, though He felt it as His own, was nevertheless spoken with a loud voice to indicate not despair, but rather

hope that the sun would rise again and scatter the darkness.[15]

Sadly, this "penal" dimension of Christ's saving work all too often has been caricatured by contemporary Catholic theologians. For example, in his book *Jesus our Redeemer*, Gerald O'Collins, SJ, summarized his objections to the theory in these words:

> Some … interpret the biblical data to mean that Jesus as a substitute was personally burdened with the sins of humanity, judged, condemned, and deservedly punished in our place; through his death he thus satisfied the divine justice and propitiated an angry God. This theology of penal substitution directly attributes Christ's passion and death to God's 'vindictiveness' rather than to human violence and cruelty. … [W]hile sometimes speaking of the divine anger (e.g. Rom 1:18; 2:5, 8; 12:19; 13: 4- 5), the NT never associates that anger with Christ's suffering and death. … Instead of needing to appease an angry deity who was 'out for blood,' Christ was sent by divine love (e.g. Rom 8:3, 32) to reconcile us with God and with one another.[16]

There are so many elements of caricature packed into a short space here that it is hard to untangle them all at once! Suffice it to say: (1) it is grossly misleading to sum up the Penal Substitution Theory of Christ's saving work on the Cross as Jesus "propitiating an angry God," since Jesus himself is God the Son Incarnate. He made a propitiatory offering of Himself

---

[15] Fulton Sheen *The Life of Christ* (The Crown Publishing Group, 1977 abridged edition), from chapters 39 and 43.

[16] Gerald O'Collins, SJ, *Jesus Our Redeemer*. Oxford: Oxford University Press, 2007, p. 177-178.

to clear our debt to His own Divine Justice, again, a divine attribute he shares with the Father and the Holy Spirit. (2) It is false to imply that our only choice lies between, on the one hand, the notion that "an angry God was out for blood" and needed to be appeased, or, on the other hand, that Christ was sent to save us "by divine love." The whole point of the doctrine of penal substitution is that as an act of merciful love for us, the divine Son Incarnate, Jesus Christ, bore the just penalty for our sins in our place on the Cross; *this was an expression of perfect Divine Justice and perfect Divine Love at the same time.* (3) While it is true that the New Testament never explicitly connects Christ's passion and death with the propitiation of God's anger or wrath, again, we need to remember that the biblical words "anger" and "wrath" are merely metaphors for Divine Justice. As we have seen earlier in this chapter, the Bible does indeed directly connect divine retributive justice with the Cross both implicitly and explicitly, for example, in the Garden of Gethsemane when Christ prayed that the "cup" might be taken away from him; in Galatians 3:13-14, which speaks of Christ becoming a "curse" for us on the tree of the Cross; and also in Isaiah 53, which speaks of the Suffering Servant of the Lord as "bearing our sins" and being "chastised" for us, and proclaims that "the Lord has laid on him the iniquity of us all." Finally, (4) The Penal Theory certainly does not "attribute Christ's passion and death to God's 'vindictiveness' rather than to human violence and cruelty." God the Father did not kill his Son; he merely permitted his Son to die at the hands of sinful men, and brought the most wonderful good out of this permitted evil. In any case, no defender of the penal aspect of redemption speaks of divine "vindictiveness;" as previously noted, this pejorative term implies a desire for retributive justice *instead of, or apart from mercy and love* — a separation which is never true of God's nature or his acts. The whole point of the penal dimension of the mystery of the Cross is that on the Cross the divine Son of God takes care of all the requirements of Divine Justice on our behalf, and thereby manifests the very depths of his merciful love for us all.[17]

Again, I believe this issue is an important one in the Church today because a vague or truncated doctrine of the Cross prevents us from clearly proclaiming something at the very heart of the gospel. And few things will weaken the effectiveness of the New Evangelization more than a muddled gospel message.

Finally, I need to reiterate here something I said in-passing before: *The atoning sacrifice that Jesus made on the Cross for our sins is only one aspect of the multi-dimensional mystery of all that the Son of God accomplished to re-unite us with the Father.* I am emphasizing this aspect of Christ's saving work in this chapter only because I find it is so often neglected in Catholic writing on the subject today. About a hundred years ago, an Anglican bishop summed up the whole matter very well when he wrote:

> There are, in fact, three relations in which our Lord stands to us in the New Testament. There is *Christ in front of us,* who sets before us the standard of the new life — in whom we see the true meaning of manhood. That is to kindle our desire. There is *Christ for us* — our propitiation or atonement — winning for us, at the price of His blood-shedding, freedom from all the guilt and bondage of the past, the assurance of free forgiveness and a fresh start. Then there is *Christ in us* — our new life by the Spirit, molding us inwardly into His likeness, and conforming us to His character. And the three are one. Each is

---

[17] This paragraph is based on a similar analysis of O'Collins' position in my book *The Incarnation: Rediscovering Kenotic Christology*, p. 538-539.

unintelligible without the others. The redeeming work of Christ lies in all together.[18]

Sacramental Confession: Where the Cross Meets Our Sins

With this theology of redemption and forgiveness in mind, let's look at the sacrament of Reconciliation. This is the special sacrament in which Jesus seeks to apply to our hearts the graces He won for us on the Cross, graces which can remove the guilt and punishment due for all sins we commit after our baptism. In short, after baptism, it's one of the principal places where, on a regular basis, on account of His saving Passion and Death He forgives our moral debt to Divine Justice, and pours into our hearts His healing, sanctifying love. In our struggle against sin, it is where we know we can always come with a contrite heart for a fresh start, receiving a renewal of divine forgiveness, and the deep refreshment of divine grace.

Jesus gave us The Holy Eucharist, too, as regular medicine for our souls, to pardon the lesser, venial sins we commit day by day, and refresh our hearts with an increase of His sanctifying grace. Indeed, the Eucharist unites us in the most intimate way with the Heart of our Savior, for in the Blessed Sacrament He not only gives us gifts and graces from the Holy Spirit, He even gives us Himself.

Whenever we go to Holy Communion, we can prepare our hearts to receive Him by calling to mind the tremendous price he paid on the Cross for our salvation, and all the healing and sanctifying graces He longs to pour out upon us in this sacrament. Borrowing some lines from the great Evangelical hymn beloved by the evangelist Billy Graham, when we

---

[18] Charles Gore, *The Reconstruction of Belief* (London: John Murray, 1926), p. 595-596.

approach the altar to receive the Body and Blood of Christ we can pray:

> Just as I am — without one plea,
> But that thy Blood was shed for me,
> And that thou bidd'st me come to thee —
> O Lamb of God, I come.

> Just as I am — though tossed about
> With many a conflict, many a doubt,
> Fightings and fears within, without —
> O Lamb of God, I come.

> Just as I am—thou wilt receive,
> Wilt welcome, pardon, cleanse, relieve —
> Because thy promise I believe,
> O Lamb of God, I come.

> Just as I am — thy love unknown
> Has broken every barrier down —
> Now to be thine, yea thine alone,
> O Lamb of God, I come.

Some of our sins are so serious, however, that they separate us from Him, and from the Holy Spirit altogether, and drive His sanctifying grace right out of our hearts. The ancient Fathers of the Church listed murder, adultery, and apostasy as the most grievous of these "mortal sins," but there are others as well, such as acts of deliberate, premeditated cruelty and malice, major acts of theft and fraud (especially victimizing the poor and needy), rape and incest, dishonesty in important matters, and willful rejection or distortion of the revealed truth of God. In the New Testament, St. Paul offered several lists of the kind of sins that can keep us from the Kingdom of God (I Cor 6:9-10; Eph 5:5; Gal 5:19-21; cf. Rev 21:8). For an act to be classed as a mortal sin, it must concern a grave matter, and be done with full understanding of its moral character, and with deliberate and free consent.[19]

Big sins indeed: but not bigger than Christ's merciful Love! As Jesus said to St. Faustina, in words he intended for all of us:

> My mercy is greater than your sins, and those of the entire world. Who can measure the extent of my goodness? For you I descended from heaven to earth; for you I allowed myself to be nailed to the cross; for you I let my Sacred Heart be pierced with a lance, thus opening wide the source of mercy for you. Come, then, with trust to draw graces from this fountain. I never reject a contrite heart. ... Sooner would heaven and earth turn into nothingness, than would my mercy fail to embrace a trusting soul. (*Diary*, entries 1485 and 1777)

To find forgiveness for such grave sins, it is important to go to Confession, because the risen Jesus promised His apostles, "If you forgive the sins of any, they are forgiven; if you retain the sins of any, they are retained" (Jn 20: 21-23). The bishops and priests are those who carry on the leadership ministry of the apostles in the Church. Being honest with God about one's sins in the privacy of the confessional, and with the help of Christ's sacramental representative, a bishop or priest, brings us the assurance of divine forgiveness and a renewal of divine grace — the very gifts that He won for us on the Cross — and for some also, badly needed relief for a troubled conscience. The *Catechism* puts it this way, in entries 1446, and 1468:

> Christ instituted the sacrament of Penance for all sinful members of His Church. Above all, for all those who since Baptism have fallen into grave sin, and have thus lost

---

[19] On this see the *Catechism*, entries 1854-1864.

their baptismal grace, and wounded ecclesial communion. It is to them that the sacrament of Penance offers a new possibility to convert and to recover the grace of justification. The Fathers of the Church present this sacrament as "The second plank of salvation after the shipwreck which is the loss of grace." ... "The whole power of the sacrament of penance consists in restoring us to God's grace, and joining us with Him in an intimate friendship." Reconciliation with God is thus the purpose and effect of this sacrament. For those who receive the sacrament of Penance with a contrite heart and religious disposition, reconciliation "is usually followed by peace and serenity of conscience, with strong spiritual consolation." Indeed the sacrament of Reconciliation with God brings about a true spiritual resurrection, restoration of the dignity and blessings of the life of the children of God, of which the most precious is friendship with God.

We need to remember that by committing mortal sins, we are betraying the One who loved us so much that He created us in His own image, and bought us with His own Blood on the Cross. The Gospel according to Saint Luke, sometimes known as "The Gospel of Mercy," portrays this with poignant beauty. There we read of our Lord's love for all people, and the tragedy that we so often let Him down — and yet, the wonder and mystery that He keeps on loving us anyway, like a good shepherd who never stops searching for His lost sheep until He finds them.

The problem that many people face today, however, is not a lack of regret or sorrow for their mortal sins. A poll came out some years ago that showed that one of the main reasons lapsed Catholics do not go to Church anymore is they feel that they are not good enough to go, that they are "too far gone," so to speak, and could not possibly be forgiven for all the bad things they have done. But the Church was not meant to be merely a place for "good" people! As someone once wisely said, the Church is not a museum for saints; it's a hospital for sinners. If you are struggling against the guilt and power of your own sins, then checking-in to "the sin hospital", a Catholic Church, is precisely where you can find the treatment and spiritual medicine that you need.

One would think that all this would be welcomed as Good News, the best possible news that sinners like us could ever hear. The divine Son of God, Jesus Christ, loved us so much that He redeemed us with the price of His own blood on the Cross, and won for us the sacraments (especially the sacraments of Baptism, Reconciliation, and the Eucharist) which apply the merits and graces of His saving death directly to our hearts. What could be better than that?

Yet many of us shy away from the confessional as something threatening, to be avoided if at all possible.

One of the great writers in the Divine Mercy movement in North America, Vinny Flynn, likes to point out the remarkable difference between our attitude toward Holy Eucharist on the one hand, and our attitude toward Confession on the other. If we say we are going to go to the Eucharist, we often say, "I want to go to Communion." And we say it with a smile. But if we tell someone we're off to the sacrament of Reconciliation, we usually say, "I *have to* go to Confession." Have to. The fact is that we tend to see the Eucharist as something joyful, refreshing, and uplifting, but Confession is something we sometimes *have to do*: something we have to get through and get over with if we have fallen into mortal sin, so that we can get to the more enjoyable thing later, which is the Eucharist. Again this attitude plagues many lapsed Catholics, too. They would not mind going to Eucharist on Sundays again; they just know that to do so with any honesty and integrity, they might have to go through a pretty serious confession first. And it's too much; it awakens their doubts and fears that they really might not be "forgivable" or lovable anymore. Moreover, they fear that they really might not be able to do any better with their lives in the future, even if the burden of the past could be wiped away. So they don't even try. Rather than set themselves up for failure and disappointment, they just stay home.

Now, in part, this hesitation is perfectly understandable. After all a sincere confession, for any of us, can be a bit painful at times. It's very humbling, even humiliating, to have to verbalize in the presence of another person (in this case, in the presence of a priest) the miserable, base, or shameful things that we sometimes do. It hurts. It uproots our pride. It's like pulling a bad tooth. Still, like having a bad tooth pulled, we know the temporary discomfort will be good for us in the end. And if we are willing to go through with it, we will hear those blessed and comforting words of absolution, pronounced over us by the priest, assuring us of the pardon of Jesus Christ, the Son of God, and we will indeed find relief for our troubled conscience, and a fresh start. Still, it's not an easy thing to do at times, especially after being away from confession for a long time. The "shame factor" can feel huge at first. And we still may wonder whether the effects of the treatment will be worth the cost in humiliation and embarrassment.

Here the *Diary* of Saint Faustina, and the *Catechism* can be of great help to us. For these two great books teach us the same thing: that the sacrament of Reconciliation is primarily about healing. It's about coming to the healing fountain of the merciful love of Jesus Christ, who will not only completely pardon us for the past, on the basis of His death on the Cross for us, but also give us the spiritual refreshment and strength we need to live a new life in the future.

We know from the *Catechism* that all the sacraments are given to us to impart God's grace to our souls. In entry 1999, for example, we find a good definition of divine grace: "The grace of Christ is the gratuitous gift [that is, the free gift] that God makes to us of His own life, infused by the Holy Spirit into our soul, to heal it of sin, and to sanctify it." This is especially true of two sacraments in particular that the *Catechism* calls "sacraments of healing" (entry 1421):

> The Lord Jesus Christ, Physician of our souls and bodies, who forgave the sins of the paralytic, and restored him to bodily health, has willed that His Church continue in the power of the Holy Spirit His own work of healing and salvation, even among her own members. This is the purpose of the two sacraments of healing: the sacrament of Penance, and the sacrament of the Anointing of the Sick.

The truth is that sin causes deep wounds and brokenness within our souls. Sin is not only a violation of God's commandments and laws, a breaking of His rules, so to speak; it also poisons and weakens our souls. Mortal sin even drives the life-giving Holy Spirit out of our hearts altogether. Thus, the sacrament of Reconciliation not only enables us to receive the assurance of God's pardon for our misdeeds on the basis of the Cross of Christ, it also enables us to receive a renewal of the life-giving Holy Spirit again, and all the sanctifying and healing graces that He wants to pour into our hearts.

If going to sacramental Confession seems like a daunting task at times, just remember that it's not only the pathway to the assurance of pardon, but also to the healing of our broken hearts. In fact the spiritual healing that this sacrament can bring to us is so amazing that, as we have seen, the *Catechism* tells us it can bring about a true, "spiritual resurrection" within us: a true Easter morning for the soul.

All of this is precisely what our Savior taught Saint Faustina Kowalska as well about this sacrament. Jesus said to her, recorded in Diary entry 1588: "Today, I am sending you with My mercy to the people of the whole world. I do not want to punish aching mankind, but I desire to heal it, pressing it to My merciful heart." That is a very revealing quote, because when our Lord starts out by saying, "I do not want to punish," we might expect Him to say, "I do not want to punish *sinful* mankind but to *forgive* it." But Jesus did not put it that way. He put the emphasis elsewhere. He said, "I do not want to punish *aching* mankind, but I desire to *heal* it." Our Savior is so compassionate. While He is certainly offended and grieved by our sins, He also sees clearly how our sins can wound and tear the very life out of our souls. In other words, He sees how mankind is "aching" from sin, and so He wants not only to *pardon* us for our sins, but to *heal* our hearts too, pressing them close to His own merciful Heart. In *Diary* entry 1487, Jesus encouraged Faustina by saying to her: "Tell Me about everything. Be sincere in dealing with Me. Reveal all the wounds of your heart, and I will heal them." As a result, Faustina always approached the confessional with childlike trust, knowing that her Savior was always there to welcome, pardon and heal her.

Perhaps the most remarkable teaching that our Lord gave to Saint Faustina about this sacrament is found in her *Diary* entry 1448. Jesus said to her:

> Write. Speak of My mercy. Tell souls where they are to look for solace; that is, in the Tribunal of Mercy, [the sacrament of Reconciliation]. There the greatest miracles take place and are incessantly repeated. To avail oneself of this miracle, it is not necessary to go on a great pilgrimage, or to carry out some external ceremony. It suffices to come with faith to the feet of My representative, and to reveal to

Him one's misery, and the miracle of Divine Mercy will be fully demonstrated. Were souls like a decaying corpse, so that from a human standpoint, there would be no hope of restoration, and everything would be already lost, it is not so with God. The miracle of Divine Mercy restores that soul in full.

Let's look more closely at those last two sentences spoken by our Lord. Remember how the *Catechism* told us that a good confession brings about a true spiritual resurrection within us, an Easter morning for the soul? That is precisely what Jesus taught Saint Faustina here as well. Even if our hearts are as dead from sin as a lifeless corpse, He says, still, the miraculous power of Divine Mercy that flows through this sacrament can restore that soul completely to new life and fresh hope.

The graces of healing that flow through this sacrament are truly amazing. In *Diary*, entry 1602, Jesus said to Saint Faustina that confession is a personal, life-giving encounter with Jesus Himself:

> Daughter, when you go to confession to this fountain of My mercy, the Blood and Water which came forth from My Heart always flows down upon your soul and ennobles it. Every time you go to confession, immerse yourself entirely in My mercy with great trust, so that I may pour the bounty of my grace upon your soul. When you approach the confessional, know this: that I Myself am waiting there for you. I'm only hidden by the priest, but I Myself act in your soul. Here the misery of the soul meets the God of mercy. Tell souls that from this fount of mercy, they draw graces solely with the vessel of trust. If their trust is great, there is no limit to my generosity. The torrents of grace inundate humble souls."

These words sound like an echo of our Savior in the gospels when He said, "Come to me, all who labor and are heavy laden, and I will give you rest. ... If anyone thirst, let him come to me and drink. He who believes in me, as the Scripture has said, 'Out of his heart shall flow rivers of living water'" (Mt 11:28; Jn 7:37-38).

In fact, as we have already seen in *Diary* entry 1448, quoted above, Jesus goes so far as to tell Saint Faustina that in this sacrament, "The greatest miracles take place and are incessantly repeated." The greatest miracles of all! Now, we are used to speaking of the miracle of the Mass, Christ's real presence in the Eucharist, and that's a pretty great miracle. Or how about the miracle of Christ's resurrection from the dead? Or how about the miracles at Lourdes, Fatima and Guadalupe? Or how about the miracle of the creation of the whole universe out of nothing? But our Lord said these are *not* the greatest miracles. The greatest miracles, He said, take place *in the confessional,* and are incessantly repeated.

How can we possibly understand this?

Saint Thomas Aquinas can give us some help here. In his great *Summa Theologiae*, Saint Thomas wrote that the miracle of the restoration and salvation of the soul is, in God's eyes, a greater miracle than the creation of the universe itself. For the material universe is something that was brought into being for a time, but one day will pass away. A soul that is saved, however, is saved for eternal life. In the case of the salvation of the soul, the *effects* of God's action last *forever*. In that sense the creation of the universe is a lesser miracle than the rescue of a single human soul.

Also, notice that all of the other great miracles that we just mentioned, (the creation of the universe, Lourdes, Fatima, Guadalupe, the Mass, even Easter itself), are caused solely by

God's power and by His will. He commands, and it is done. But it is not so with the rescue and healing of a human soul. God will not overwhelm a soul by His power. He will not force us to repent. Indeed, He *cannot* compel us to repent if our reconciliation with Him is to be a free response by His human creatures. If God overpowered our human freedom with His grace, *compelling* us to repent and be healed, then He would be making us into mere puppets on a string, and not into real friends of God who freely return His love. He does not want to turn us into mere puppets or robots. He wants His long lost friends *freely* to return to Him, and to rejoice in His love. So, for God to convert a sinner and bring him home to Heaven is an even greater achievement than any of His other miracles. It requires all His wisdom, all His loving skill, *without using force*, to call, to strengthen, and to guide lost sinners home to His Heart. The healing and restoration of a human soul, therefore, especially through sacramental Confession, is the greatest miracle of His merciful love.

Let's go back again to *Diary* entry 1448. There is one more thing that Jesus told Sister Faustina about the mystery of this sacrament that we should not pass over without comment. Jesus said to her, "Tell souls where they are to look for solace, that is, in the Tribunal of Mercy": in other words, the sacrament of Reconciliation. It was from Vinny Flynn, the Divine Mercy evangelist, that I first heard this properly explained. He once pointed out that "Tribunal of Mercy" almost sounds like a contradiction in terms, like saying "hot ice". After all for most of us the word "tribunal" conjures up in our minds anything but an expectation mercy! Rather, it makes us think of a court room scene, with judges sitting in high-backed chairs, looking very severe and displeased, whose job it is to make an inquiry into a serious criminal charge, and to pronounce a verdict according to the most stringent principles of justice. In other words, if you get called to appear before a "tribunal," it's usually because you're in big trouble!

Yet our Lord calls the sacrament of Reconciliation a tribunal of "mercy." How can this be?

This kind of language only makes sense, if we remember who the judges are that are sitting on this tribunal. If the confessional is anything like a courtroom scene, then it is really the court of Heaven we are kneeling before, awaiting our sentence. And the only judges in that courtroom are the Father, the Son, and the Holy Spirit — The Holy Trinity of Divine Mercy — they are the "tri" in this tribunal. That is why, when the priest pronounces the absolution, He starts with these words: "God the Father of mercies, through the Resurrection of His Son, sent the Holy Spirit ...." It is the Holy Trinity who is actually waiting for us in this sacrament, ready to apply the remedy of His merciful love to our sin-sick souls.

In short, the throne of God's justice, through Christ's sacrifice upon the Cross, has become for us even more the throne of His grace. He fulfilled the demands of Divine Justice on the Cross in order to open the floodgates of His grace and mercy upon us — especially through the sacraments of Baptism, Reconciliation, and the Eucharist. As the book of Hebrews puts it in chapter 4, beginning at verse 15: "For we have not a high priest, who is unable to sympathize with our weaknesses, but one who in every respect has been tempted as we are, yet without sinning. Let us then with confidence draw near to the throne of grace, that we may receive mercy and find grace to help in time of need." We do not have a high priest — that is, Jesus Christ — who is unable to "sympathize" with us in our weakness as we struggle against our besetting sins. The great Church Father, St. Irenaeus of Lyons, put it best when he said that our Heavenly Father always reaches out to us with His two loving arms, His Son and His Spirit, to embrace us with His merciful love. That's the gospel in a nutshell. It is cause for rejoicing indeed, just as the father in Christ's parable, the Prodigal Son, rejoiced when He welcomed His lost son home: "It was fitting to make merry and be glad, for this your brother was dead, and is alive; he was lost, and is found."(Lk 15: 32).

It follows that whenever we make a good and sincere confession, we not only find the joy of forgiveness, and new life for ourselves; in addition, we actually cause the glorified Heart of Jesus to rejoice. As St. Luke's gospel tells us, whenever the Good Shepherd finds His lost sheep, He puts them on His shoulders and brings them home "rejoicing" (Lk 15:5-6; Mt 18:12-14). Jesus explained this to Saint Faustina, too, as recorded in her *Diary* in entries 1486, and 1489:

> What joy fills my heart when you return to me. Because you are weak, I take you in My arms and carry you to the home of My Father. ... In a soul that lives on My love alone, I reign as in Heaven. I watch over it day and night. In it I find My happiness. My ear is attentive to reach request of its heart. ... O child, especially beloved by Me, apple of My eye, rest a moment near My heart, and taste of the love in which you will delight for all eternity.

This joy that our Good Shepherd experiences whenever He recues one of His lost sheep actually tells us something very important about His Heart. We commonly say that "Jesus loves us in spite of our sins." And we understand that to mean that He pardons us when we are contrite and confess, He helps us in our struggles, and He puts up with us with great patience. No doubt all that is true as far as it goes, but the Gospels tell us even more. Our Lord is even more closely bonded to us than that. He actually "likes" us. In other words, He has *boundless affection* for us. He feels for us when we are suffering and lost, and rejoices for us whenever He is able to relieve and restore us. Notice that the passage from Hebrews, quoted above, says that He "sympathizes" with us. Again, when He finds His lost sheep, Saint Luke's gospel tells us, He puts them on His shoulders and brings them home "rejoicing." In short, Jesus Christ not only loves us with the virtue of charity, He also feels for our plight in the depths of His Heart with tender affection.

How is this possible? How can our Savior have such tender affection for us when we so often fall into sin — when our souls are so often wounded by the corruption of habitual sin? How can He like us when we are so often "unlikeable"?

Again, St. Thomas Aquinas can shed some light on this matter for us. In his writings Saint Thomas asked the question, "Why does God love sinners despite their sins?" The answer that St. Thomas gave is that God does not so much love us because of anything we have done, or have not done; rather God loves us because of our *potential*. With the help of His grace we are creatures capable of eternal beatitude — as St. Thomas put it in Latin, *capax beatitudo*. In other words, our Lord always looks past our imperfect deeds to *what we always have the potential to become: saints of His merciful Heart*. You know how terrific a child can feel if a parent, teacher, or athletics coach turns to that child and says, "You've got potential, kid." Well, in God's eyes, we all have potential because He made us in His image and God doesn't make junk. That is the underlying reason why God loves us in spite of all our sins: because He knows that until the day we die, we still have the potential to surrender to His grace and become saints full-to-overflowing with His merciful love.

That is also the reason why Jesus our Savior retains such boundless affection for us, even when we wander far from Him. He sees our hidden potential underneath the grit and the grime. It is a pearl of grace price to Him.

So, whenever we come to Jesus in sacramental confession, we not only fulfill God's just requirement for obtaining pardon for our sins, and we not only find in this sacrament a fountain of mercy, where healing graces for our hearts always flow. In addition to all that, we actually cause the merciful Heart of Jesus to rejoice, a Heart that so often has been wounded by the sins of thankless men and women.

Finally: what has made all the joy and healing from this sacrament available to us? The clue is in what the priest does in the confessional at the very moment he absolves us of our sins: he makes the sign of the Cross. Everything about this sacrament of mercy, in fact, is based on what Christ accomplished for us on Calvary. It was there that he paid the price for our forgiveness: that is, for the pardon of our sins and for all the graces we need for salvation. As St. Paul wrote: "And you, who were dead in trespasses ... God made alive together with [Christ], having forgiven all our trespasses, having cancelled the bond which stood against us with its legal demands; this he set aside, nailing it to the cross" (Col 2:13-14).[20] So the confessional is where the Cross of our Savior meets our sins, and the Cross is where the debt of those sins was paid by our Savior. It's perfect Divine Love rescuing us in accord with perfect Divine Justice.

---

[20] *The Ignatius Catholic Study Bible* (2010 edition), p. 368, offers some helpful comments on the meaning of verse 14 here: "the bond: a list of charges filed against the sinful human family. Christ destroyed this legal certificate on the Cross, when he cancelled our debt of guilt and won pardon for our crimes. Paul is probably thinking of the Mosaic Law, which, as the written expression of God's precepts, pronounces divine curses upon sin (Dt 27:15-26). In this scheme, Jesus mounted the Cross to bear the curses of the Old Covenant so that the blessings of the New could flow forth to the world (Gal 3:13-14)."

Chapter Three
Purgatory: Place of Punishment or Process of Healing?

For Catholics born and raised before Vatican II, the mere mention of Purgatory may cause a shudder. All too often in those days, Catholic children were taught that Purgatory is a frightening place of flames and torment, a temporary hell for those who were not quite bad enough to merit even worse punishment.

For Catholics born and raised after Vatican II, on the other hand, Purgatory is generally no big deal. All too often they have been taught that Purgatory is simply a place of final spiritual healing in which souls gently float upward on the last stage of their journey toward the Light of God.

These two perspectives may seem like polar opposites, but they actually have something very important in common (and if you have read the first two chapters of this book, you can guess what that is): they are both dead wrong — excuse the pun. The first sees Purgatory solely as a place of punishment, where God exercises His justice on the imperfectly penitent. The second sees Purgatory solely as a process of spiritual purification, designed by God's merciful love to prepare us for Heaven. Both perspectives are true as far as they go — but dead wrong if taken as the whole truth about Purgatory on their own.

To sort out the confusion, let's begin at the beginning. In other words, let's ask: Why should we believe that there is a Purgatory at all?

As we shall see, Scripture, Catholic Tradition, the Magisterium, and rational common sense all come together

in support of this doctrine. At the same time, we need to
bear in mind that Purgatory is one of the mysteries of
divine revelation. That does not mean we are completely
"in the dark" about it; it simply means that there is more to
this mystery than we can possibly fathom in this life. Thus,
it is not surprising that down through history different
streams of Christianity have developed somewhat different
ideas about it.

The Purgatory Consensus, East and West

Roman Catholics and Eastern Orthodox Christians (e.g.
Greek and Russian Orthodox) have much in common
regarding the whole matter of Purgatory and prayers for
the departed. For example, both traditions find a
foundation for such prayers in Holy Scripture. In 2
Maccabees 12:42-46, the Jewish hero Judas Maccabeus
ordered sacrifices to be offered in the Temple for the souls
of his soldiers killed in battle so that their sins might be
forgiven: "It is therefore a holy and wholesome thought to
pray for the dead, that they may be loosed from their sins"
(verse 46, Douay-Rheims translation). Obviously, if they
could be "loosed" from their sins after their death by the
prayers of the living, they must be in some kind of post-
mortem state in which cleansing or release from sin is
possible. This seems to have been a common Jewish belief
in the century before Christ.[1]

---

[1] Some Protestant apologists claim that the Catholic Church only
added the two books of Maccabees to the Scriptures in 1546, at
the Council of Trent, to counter Martin Luther's contention that
prayers for the departed were not found in the Bible. This claim
is demonstrably false. The Maccabean corpus was accepted at
Rome as canonical Scripture as early as 496 A.D., in a Decree of
Pope St. Gelasius. These books also were listed as canonical
Scripture by the ecumenical Council of Florence (1439-1443)

In his book *Prayers and Practices for the Souls in Purgatory*, Fr. Dan Cambra, MIC, writes that Christ's parable of The Rich Man and Lazarus in Luke 16:19-31 gives us strong evidence for the existence of an intermediate state between Heaven and hell before the death and resurrection of Jesus. He explains:

> Basically, what we have in this parable is that a rich man and a poor man die. The rich man goes to a place of infernal fiery torment, while the poor man Lazarus rests quietly with Abraham. There is a huge abyss that one can't cross over between where the rich man suffers in flames and where Lazarus enjoys a place of rest. This place of rest was where the souls of the saints of the Old Testament awaited the arrival of Jesus.

> Sometimes people ask, "What was this place of rest?" Well, it was clearly not Heaven, because Christ is the one who is telling the parable [i.e., without Jesus present, there is no Heaven]. ... The place of rest in this parable must have been an intermediate place between Heaven and hell, which the Jews referred to as "Sheol." Sheol was not quite the same as Purgatory because both the righteous and unrighteous would go to Sheol, but it was very close in meaning. ...[I]n 1 Peter 3:19-20 we hear of the place to which Jesus "went

---

long before the Reformation. The decree on the scriptural canon at the Council of Trent only clarified remaining uncertainties about some of the Old Testament "Deuterocanonical" books because the status of a few of the books in that group were still in dispute — but I and II Maccabees were not among those disputed texts in the Catholic world.

[after His death] and preached to the souls in prison."[2]

In his encyclical letter *Spe Salvi* (2007), Pope Benedict XVI explained further that in ancient Jewish belief, the "idea of an intermediate state includes the view that these souls are not simply in a sort of temporary custody, but, as the parable of the rich man illustrates, are already being punished or are experiencing a provisional form of bliss" (section 44). In other words, what we have in the Parable of the Rich Man and Lazarus is a portrait of a kind of pre-Purgatory before the death and resurrection of Christ, a state intermediate between Heaven and hell.

The New Testament also contains indirect allusions to prayer for the departed after the resurrection of Jesus Christ. Saint Paul mentions in 1 Corinthians 15:29 an ancient practice in which Christians were "baptized on behalf of the dead." This may have been an early, and somewhat extravagant form of liturgical prayer for the departed. Also possible: St. Paul was using the word "baptism" in this passage metaphorically (as in Mk 10:38), to refer to the baptism of earthly trials, mortifications, and afflictions accepted and offered up on behalf of the departed by the early Christians. In Colossians 1:24, for example, St. Paul mentions his own practice of offering up his sufferings for the good of the Church. In any case, he does not criticize prayers and offerings for the departed in 1 Corinthians 15, and implicitly his argument in that chapter approves of them, for he points to the Corinthians own practice of "baptism" on behalf of the dead as proof

[2] Fr. Dan Cambra, MIC, *Prayers and Practices for the Souls in Purgatory* (Stockbridge, MA: Marian Press, 2017), p. 21-22.

that they share with him the ultimate hope of final resurrection for all faithful Christian believers.[3]

In 2 Timothy 1:16-18, St. Paul wrote of his friend Onesiphorous: "May the Lord grant unto him to find the mercy of the Lord on that day" (that is, the Day of Judgment). The context of St. Paul's remarks suggests that Onesiphorous was already dead (see 2 Tm 1:18 and 4:19).

In addition, there are several passages in the New Testament which speak of the praises of God being offered from those "under the earth." Fr. Cambra explains what this implies:

> Now I'd like to share with you three passages from the New Testament, which refer to three levels of reality. The first is Philippians 2:1-10: "That at the name of Jesus every knee should bow, in heaven and on earth and under the earth, and every tongue confess that Jesus Christ is Lord, to the glory of God the Father." Similarly, in Revelation 5:3, we read "and no one in heaven or on earth or under the earth was able to open the scroll or look into it." And further, Revelation 5:13: "And I heard every creature in heaven and on earth and under the earth and in the sea and all therein saying, "To him who sits upon the throne and to the Lamb be blessing and honor and glory and might for ever and ever."

---

[3] In fact, as, St. Francis De Sales once pointed out, there is a verbal similarity between 2 Maccabees 12:44 and I Cor 15:29.This makes it likely that St. Paul was appealing to a common Christian belief in his day of the efficacy of prayers for the dead as a sign of universal Christian belief in everlasting life. See Cambra, MIC, *Prayers and Practices for the Souls in Purgatory*, p.23

Obviously, two levels of this three-tiered reality (all those "in heaven" and "on earth") refer to the Church Triumphant and the Church Militant. But what about those referred to as "under the earth"? The reference is certainly not to those in hell. They would not be praising God. But who else would be praising God? By the process of elimination, it must be referring to the Church Suffering in Purgatory.[4]

We will look at more evidence from the New Testament for the existence of Purgatory later in this chapter.

We also have indications from outside of the New Testament that prayer for the departed was apostolic teaching and practice. Saint Polycarp, for example, who was martyred in 156 A.D., had learned the faith in his boyhood from St. John the Apostle himself. In the 2nd century account of his martyrdom, we find that just before his death, he prayed "for all those whom he had ever known." Given that Polycarp was 86 at the time of his execution, most of those whom he had ever known must have been dead. In the *Acts of Paul and Thecla* (ca. 160 AD), a woman named Tryphaena asks Thecla to become her surrogate daughter. Tryphaena's own deceased daughter had appeared to her in a dream asking for prayers: "Mother, you shall have this stranger Thecla in my place, in order that she may pray concerning me, and that I may be transferred to the place of the just." In *The Martyrdom of Perpetua and Felicitias* (ca. 203 AD), Perpetua receives a vision of her deceased brother Dinocrates in a place of gloom and suffering: "But I trusted that my prayer would bring help to his suffering; and I prayed for him every day .... Then ... I saw that that place which I had formerly

---

[4] Ibid., p. 24.

observed to be in gloom was now bright, and Dinocrates, with a clean body well clad, was finding refreshment." Abercius, Bishop of Hieropolis (d. 167 AD) had inscribed on his tomb the plea: "May everyone ... pray for Abercius." Notable Christian writers from the early third century also endorsed the practice of praying for the departed:

> [T]he early Church author Tertullian, writing around A.D. 211, mentions, "We offer sacrifices for the dead on their birthday anniversaries" (*The Crown*, 3:3). This is a reference to the day they died — the day they were born into eternal life. Clearly, the early Church recognized a need for suffrages for the faithful departed.[5] ...

> We can also look to Origen, who, in a homily on Jeremiah given around A.D. 244, points out that 'if a man departs this life with lighter faults, he is condemned to a fire which burns away the lighter materials, and prepares the soul for the kingdom of God, where nothing defiled may enter'....[6]

Also, in the Roman catacombs, where the early Christians of that city buried their dead, we find a number of third century inscriptions requesting prayers for the departed.

In short, given the widespread practice of prayers for the

---

[5] By "offering sacrifices" here Tertullian meant offering up the sacrifice of the Holy Eucharist on their behalf. In his work *de Monogamia*, X, Tertullian writes of someone who had lost her husband, "She prays for his soul, and seeks refreshment for him in the middle place."

[6] Cited in Cambra, *Prayers and Practices for the Souls in Purgatory*, p. 27.

faithful departed among Christians of the second and early third centuries — without any controversy or debate on the matter — it hardly seems likely that entire Christian community throughout the world had deviated from apostolic teaching in this regard.

In fact, the most ancient liturgical texts for the Eucharist that we possess, both from the eastern and the western Mediterranean, also contain prayers for the departed. A liturgy from the fourth century attributed to the Apostle James, for example, contains the prayer, "We commemorate all the faithful dead who have died in the true faith …. We ask, we entreat, we pray Christ our God, who took their souls and spirits to Himself, that by His many compassions He will make them worthy of the pardon of their faults and the remission of their sins."[7]

As we shall see throughout this chapter, many early Fathers of the Church also mention this practice. Saint Clement of Alexandria (d. 215 AD)[8] may have been the first of the Fathers to do so. He was followed in the same century by St. Cyprian of Carthage (d. 258), and later, for example, by St. John Chrysostom (d. 407), who remarks that saying prayers for the faithful departed was a duty passed down from the apostles themselves.[9] St. Augustine of Hippo (d. 430) was one of the strongest advocates of this practice:

---

[7] Syriac Liturgy of St. James, "Prayers for the Dead," *Catholic Encyclopedia* (1908), cited in John Salza, *The Biblical Basis for Purgatory* (Charlotte: Saint Benedict Press, 2009), p. 147.

[8] *Stromata* 6:14 (written sometime before 202 AD).

[9] Saint Chrysostom speaks of it as a "law laid down by the Apostles" in his commentary on Philippians (I, 4, P.G., LXII, 203).

But by the prayers of the holy Church, and by the salvific sacrifice [i.e., Holy Eucharist], and by the alms which are given for their spirits, there is no doubt that the dead are aided, that the Lord might deal more mercifully with them than their sins would deserve. *The whole Church observes this practice which was handed down by the Fathers*: that it prays for those who have died in the communion of the Body and Blood of Christ, when they are commemorated in their own place in the sacrifice itself; and the sacrifice is offered also in memory of them, on their behalf. If, then, works of mercy are celebrated for the sake of those who are being remembered, who would hesitate to recommend them, on whose behalf prayers to God are not offered in vain? It is not at all to be doubted that such prayers are of profit to the dead; but for such of them as lived before their death in a way that makes it possible for these things to be useful to them after death. (Sermons, 172:2)[10]

In fact, there are no known opponents of prayers for the departed among orthodox Christian believers in the ancient Church.

The cumulative force of the evidence from the early Church, therefore, strongly suggests that prayer for the departed was an apostolic teaching and practice — and implicit in that practice and belief is another one: that we can help the departed in some way by our prayers, the faithful departed at least. If they are in hell, of course, they are beyond any help. If they are in Heaven, they do not need our help. Only if some of them are in a kind of

---

[10] Cited in Cambra, *Prayers and Practices for the Souls in Purgatory*, p. 29; italics mine.

intermediate state of final cleansing and purification does the practice of praying for the departed make any sense.

Thus far, Catholics and many Eastern Orthodox Christians are of a common mind.

Some Protestants fear that if we pray for the dead, then that implies that people have "second chances" beyond the grave to repent and come to saving faith. And if that is true — that we all get second, third, and more chances beyond this life — then why should missionaries and evangelists bother to expend their energies and risk their lives spreading the gospel among the living? After all, if people do not turn their hearts to Christ in this present life, they can always do so in the next. The doctrine of Purgatory, so understood, would undermine the urgency and importance of Christian evangelism (an urgency and importance on full display in the lives of the apostles themselves in the New Testament).

However, this represents a misunderstanding of the Catholic and Orthodox doctrine of the "intermediate state" or Purgatory. We do not intend to pray for all the departed, including those who died without repentance for mortal sin, but only for the faithful departed: that is, for those who died in faith, in a state of grace, yet who were not fully sanctified in faith, hope, and love at the time of their passing. If some Catholic prayers for the departed seem indiscriminate, that is simply because the Church on earth does not presume to judge which persons did not die in a state of grace, and were thereby eternally lost (for whom such prayers would be useless). The state of the heart at the time of death is usually known only to God. All mainstream Christian traditions accept that the underlying decision for or against Christ must be made in this present life. But as Catholic theologian Brett Salkeld put it, Catholics and Eastern Orthodox Christians generally believe that "Those who have chosen to follow Christ, but who have not yet succeeded in letting his offer of sanctifying grace penetrate into every aspect of their lives, will have the opportunity to do so after death."[11]

By praying for the departed, Catholics simply ask our Lord to complete the work that He began in those who are united to Him in faith, but whose hearts were not fully sanctified at the time of their death. For those who died with at least a tiny spark in their hearts of faith in the God of mercy (faith the size of a mustard seed, so to speak), our prayer is that the Lord in His tender mercy will fan that spark into flame in the next life, burning away as swiftly as possible the imperfections of their souls and making them ever more deeply united with Christ, "for He is like a refiner's fire, and He shall purify the sons of Levi, that they may offer unto the Lord, an offering in righteousness" (Mal 3:2, KJV). As C.S. Lewis wrote in his book *A Grief Observed* at the death of his beloved wife Joy:

> [She] was a splendid thing; a soul straight, bright, and tempered like a sword. But not a perfected saint. A sinful woman married to a sinful man; two of God's patients not yet cured. I know there are not only tears to be dried but stains to be scoured. The sword will be made even brighter. But Oh God, tenderly, tenderly.[12]

Many Evangelical Christians are convinced that God

---

[11] Brett Salkeld, *Can Catholics and Evangelicals Agree about Purgatory and the Last Judgment?* (New York: Paulist Press, 2011), p. 15.

[12] C.S. Lewis, *A Grief Observed* (London: Faber and Faber, 1966 edition), p. 37.

finishes the sanctification of every faithful soul in an instant, at the moment of death. Of course, it is possible that a soul can attain a complete surrender to the love and mercy of God at the last moment, so that nothing more needs to be done to prepare that soul for heavenly glory. This certainly seems to be what happened with the Good Thief on Calvary (Lk 23:42-43). But we have no promise in the Bible or early Christian Tradition that this happens with all of the faithful departed. In addition, this notion contradicts our experience in this present life of what profound growth in holiness usually entails. Salkeld writes:

> Sanctification obviously takes place in time during our earthly lives. How that is reflected post-mortem is not an easy question. If Evangelicals consider the problem of incomplete sanctification, many will posit that its completion will happen at the moment of death so that entry into heaven is not "delayed."... Catholics affirm that anything that can be called a "process" requires something like *time*, but do not insist that such time would be experienced as time in this life is experienced. ... In other words, while there is no use discussing one's time in purgatory according to earth's calendars, some sort of time does seem philosophically necessary for change, and for most of us, perfection would constitute significant change.[13]

---

[13] Salkeld, *Can Catholics and Evangelicals Agree about Purgatory and the Last Judgment?*, p. 15-16. Pope Benedict XVI said something similar in *Spe Salvi*, section 47: "It is clear that we cannot calculate the 'duration' of this transforming burning in terms of the chronological measurements of this world. The transforming 'moment' of this encounter [with Christ's love] eludes earthly time-reckoning — it is the heart's time, it is the time of 'passage' to communion with God in the Body of Christ."

Again, in all this Catholics and many Eastern Orthodox Christians are often in full accord. We continue to pray for the departed, entrusting their souls into the hands of our heavenly Father, that they might find continual growth in His love, until they attain what the Book of Hebrews calls "that holiness without which no one shall see the Lord" (Heb 12:14). Our Lord Jesus Himself stated that unless our righteousness exceeds that of the scribes and Pharisees, we shall not enter the Kingdom of Heaven (Mt 3:20). Since even with the help of divine grace, few of us have attained that degree of righteousness by the time of our death, our Lord provides for us a time of healing and purgation, to complete the work of sanctification in us that He started here on earth.[14] Long ago, St. Gregory of Nyssa (d. 394 AD) summed up what remains the ecumenical consensus on Purgatory:

> For [God], the one goal is this, the perfection of the universe through each man individually, the fulfillment of our nature. Some of us are purged of evil in this life, some are cured of it through fire in the after-life .... The different degrees of virtue and vice in our life will

---

[14] In her otherwise excellent book *Praying with the Saints for the Holy Souls in Purgatory* (Huntingdon, IN: Our Sunday Visitor Press, 2009), p. 43, author Susan Tassone quotes Fr. Edward McNamara that the soul in Purgatory "cannot increase in sanctity but only purify those imperfections which impede its definitive entrance into glory." Besides the implicit self-contradiction here (how can purification of those imperfections which prevent us from fully uniting with the Love of God not amount to a process of sanctification?), this teaching does not fit well with Heb 12:14, and *Catechism of the Catholic Church*, entry 1030. In any case, it is a speculation of theologians, not a definitive teaching of the Catholic Church.

be revealed in participating more quickly or more slowly in the blessedness we hope for …. The healing of the soul will be purification from evil, and this cannot be accomplished without suffering.[15]

More recently, Fr. Aidan Nichols, OP, put it this way in his book Rome and the Eastern Churches:

> At its most fundamental, the doctrine of purgatory affirms that for those who die with their wills set towards charity, further transformation is possible beyond death as a preparation for heaven. And stated thus, the doctrine is an ecumenical doctrine, which belongs to the Greek and Latin churches, no matter what terminology is used.[16]

There is one aspect of the doctrine of Purgatory, however, on which Catholics and Eastern Orthodox Christians have never really been in full accord.

Purgatory and Divine Justice

All who die in God's grace and friendship, but still imperfectly purified, are indeed assured of their eternal salvation but after death they undergo purification, so as to achieve that holiness necessary to enter the joy of heaven.
— *Catechism of the Catholic Church*, 1030

---

[15] St. Gregory of Nyssa, *De Anima et Resurrectione*, cited in Salkeld, *Can Catholics and Evangelicals Agree about Purgatory and the Last Judgment?*, p. 40. It should be noted that St. Gregory believed that *all* imperfect souls, even the most sinful, go through this purgation process, and ultimately make it to Heaven.
[16] Aidan Nichols, OP, *Rome and the Eastern Churches*, (Collegeville, MN: The Liturgical Press, 1992), p. 257.

Stated in its simplest form, as the Catechism does in entry 1030 (above), the doctrine of Purgatory is "common ground" between Catholicism and Eastern Orthodoxy. The trouble begins, however, when we unpack what each side means by the nature of the "purification" that happens in this intermediate state between earth and heaven. The ecumenical Council of Lyons of 1274, for example, defined that purification process as follows:

> If those who are truly penitent die in charity before they have done sufficient penance for their sins of omission and commission, their souls are cleansed after death in purgatorial or *cleansing punishments*.

So Purgatory is not only for the further healing and sanctification of the soul, but also for the completion of "penance" and cleansing "punishments." The ecumenical Council of Florence of 1439 was equally clear:

> And if they are truly penitent and die in God's love before having satisfied by worthy fruits of penance for their sins of commission and omission, their souls are cleansed after death by *purgatorial penalties*. In order that they be relieved from such penalties, the acts of intercession of the living benefit them, namely the sacrifices of the Mass, prayers, alms, and other works of piety which the faithful are wont to do for the other faithful, according to the Church's practice.

It is this "penal" or "judicial" side of the purification process in Purgatory that seems to be absent from Eastern Orthodox teaching — and, indeed, from most Catholic teaching on Purgatory today as well! But as we shall see, this aspect of purgatorial purification also has its roots in Scripture, and in the ancient Fathers, and (as we have just seen) it is also the teaching of two ecumenical councils of the Church. Thus, Catholics are duty bound to accept and try to understand this much neglected aspect of the mystery of Purgatory, even if we think that the emphasis should be placed elsewhere, that is, on Purgatory as a state of spiritual healing and sanctification — which is certainly what the *Catechism* stresses today.[17]

First, let's look at what is implied in Scripture concerning the penal aspect of Purgatory. In II Maccabees 12:42-46, Judas Maccabeus ordered prayers and sacrifices to be offered to the Lord for His slain soldiers to make "atonement" for them, "that they may be delivered from their sin," biblical phrases surely implying that they still needed to find a measure of divine pardon for those sins.

Jesus once said, "For with the judgment you pronounce you will be judged, and the measure you give will be the measure you get" (Mt 7:2). In other words, what goes around comes around! But where is this supposed to take place? Surely, Jesus knew that in this life the cruel and merciless often go unpunished for their crimes. Perhaps He was referring instead only to those who will suffer eternal loss in hell? But what about those who were merciless to others at times, and yet attained in this life at least an imperfect and half-hearted repentance for their

---

[17] In fact, even ecumenical councils of the Church, such as Lyons and Florence, sometimes can truly express the Church's teachings in ways that are somewhat imbalanced, needing further clarification and "rounding out" so to speak, by future authoritative magisterial teachings, such as the *Catechism*. That is not to say that those councils were wrong: their definitions of doctrine are at least "true as far as they go," and need to be taken on board. But their teachings are not necessarily the whole story.

sins? Will they be sent to hell along with the utterly wicked and unrepentant? — or will they receive a blanket divine pardon and a free ticket to Heaven after their death? Half-hearted penitents that they are, they still have some measure of moral debt owing to God — and clearing that remaining moral debt is precisely what is supposed to happen in Purgatory.[18]

Quite often Protestant theologians will object to this penal aspect of the doctrine of Purgatory on the grounds that it allegedly detracts from the efficacy of Christ's saving work. Jesus died on the Cross to take away the sins of believers completely, and once and for all, they insist: that means all of the penalty and punishment due to them is washed away by the blood of Christ. To be clear, the Catholic Church certainly does not deny this, but in the New Testament, the benefits of Christ's sacrifice on the Cross are promised to those who repent in faith. The real question is, "What about those whose repentance and faith in this life was weak and half-hearted, those who died in what the Church calls a state of 'imperfect contrition' for sin"? For example, some people are contrite more out of fear of hell or disgust with themselves, than out of love for God and sorrow at having let Him down. Are these persons, at the time of their death, suddenly and fully united to Jesus Christ and to all the benefits of His redeeming sacrifice? Do they receive a blanket pardon for all their moral debts to God at that moment? Affirmative answers to these questions would seem to involve a direct violation of Matthew 7:2 (above), and of the holiness and justice of God.

---

[18] Unfortunately, in his otherwise outstanding book *Can Catholics and Evangelicals agree about Purgatory and the Last Judgment?*, Brett Salkeld endorses the trend in modern Catholic Theology that "has moved away from any teaching regarding souls suffering expiatory pains" in Purgatory (p.67).

Ordinarily — apart from certain extraordinary acts of Divine Mercy (such as an adult baptism, or the reception of Holy Communion in a state of grace on Divine Mercy Sunday) — the merits and spiritual benefits of Christ's saving death on the Cross can only *fully* apply to those who are *fully and deeply repentant for their sins, rooted in deep faith in Christ and authentic love for Him* (e.g. Gal 5:6). Hence the need to do penance for one's sins in this life in a way that effects this deeper, inner transformation, and if that penance is not complete before death, to deepen one's penitence and love, and expiate one's remaining moral debt to God in the purifying fires of Purgatory. As Catholic apologist F.J. Sheed once wrote: "Purgatory does nothing for us that only Christ's blood can do; it simply removes the obstacles that we have interposed to the cleansing power of his blood."[19]

Let's continue with Scripture. Our Lord said, "And whoever says a word against the Son of Man will be forgiven, but whoever speaks against the Holy Spirit will not be forgiven, either in this age or the age to come" (Mt 12:32). In his book *Charity for the Holy Souls*, Fr. John Nageleisen tells us:

> From these words SS. Augustine [*De Civ. Dei*, lib. 21, c.13], Gregory the Great [*Dialogue* 4, c. 39], Bernard, Bede, and others conclude as follows... [this passage] proves convincingly that certain sins are forgiven in the next world. Now this forgiveness is not obtainable in heaven, because sin does not gain admittance there [Rev 21:27], nor in hell, whence there is no redemption.

---

[19] F.J. Sheed, *Theology for Beginners* (Cincinnati, OH: Servant Books, third edition, 1981), p. 169.

There is only one possibility: These sins are forgiven in purgatory — hence, there is a purgatory.[20]

Elsewhere in the gospels, Jesus exhorts His hearers to settle their accounts in this life, lest we be delivered to the Judge, who will cast us in prison: "Truly, I say to you, you will never get out until you have paid the last penny" (Mt 5:25-26). This is repeated in His parable in Matthew chapter 18: 32-35, where He adds, "So also my heavenly father will do to every one of you, if you do not forgive your brother from your heart." On this Nageleisen writes: "Many holy Fathers, among them Origen, St. Jerome, St. Ambrose, and others, declare that this passage is to be understood not as referring to a place of eternal punishment [hell], but to one of temporal punishment in the next world, because deliverance is promised to those who repay the last farthing."[21] As there is no deliverance at all from hell, and none needed from Heaven, it is likely that Jesus was referring here, at least implicitly, to an intermediate state where one can make up one's remaining moral debt to Divine Justice.

The most intriguing passage in the New Testament in this regard, however, comes from St. Paul's First Epistle to the Corinthians, chapter 3, verses 11-15:

For no one can lay another foundation but that which is laid: which is Christ Jesus. Now if any man builds upon this foundation gold, silver, precious   stones, wood, hay, stubble, every man's work will be manifest: for the day   of the Lord shall declare it, because it shall be

---

[20] Fr. John A. Nageleisen, *Charity for the Suffering* Souls (Rockford, IL; TAN, 1977 reprint of 1895 edition), p. 28-29. NB: by "forgiveness" here the author means "fully pardoned for sin."
[21] Ibid., p. 29.

revealed in fire, and the fire shall try every man's work, of what sort it is. If any man's work abides, which he hath built upon, he shall receive a reward. If any man's work burn, he shall suffer loss; but he himself shall be saved, yet so as by fire.

This is a difficult passage to interpret, but it seems to have been the unanimous testimony of the ancient Fathers of the Latin-speaking churches — for example, St. Cyprian, St. Ambrose, St. Jerome, St. Augustine, and St. Gregory the Great — that the metaphorical "flames" referred to here are the flames suffered by souls as a result of their particular judgment, immediately after their death. Some people build their lives upon the right "foundation" (which is faith in Christ, according to verse 11), yet they live out that faith only in very imperfect ways. Their good works are mixed with many lesser sins, which is why St. Paul says their works consist merely of "wood, hay, or stubble." After their death, these deeds are tried and burned up (so to speak) in the fires of God's judgment (verse 13).

Their works, therefore, burn up in that fire. In other words, they are condemned. But of course, "work" cannot actually "burn." That is why St. Paul clarifies in verse 15 that if any man's works burn "he shall suffer loss." This is not the loss of eternal damnation, however, for St. Paul goes on to say "but he himself shall be saved, yet so as by fire."

Some Protestant Bible scholars say that this phrase merely means "he shall be saved out of the midst of fire," which is certainly a possible reading of the text here on grammatical grounds. That would imply that this passage is talking about the final Judgment Day, as the soul escapes the judgment of his works on the Last Day without being scorched by the flames of divine judgment himself. But such is not the probable meaning of the passage, given the unanimous testimony of the Western Fathers of the Church (along with a few of the Eastern Fathers, as we shall see).

Moreover, it is hard for the Protestant reading of this passage to make sense of verse 15: "he shall suffer loss." What can this suffering and loss be? Are souls on the final Judgment Day to go weeping into heaven, suffering loss in the sense of penitential sorrow because of their imperfect works and imperfect repentance during their time on earth? There is no hint in Scripture of such a spectacle on the Last Day. It seems more likely that the traditional reading of the Latin Fathers is the correct one here: The passage refers not to the final Judgment Day, but to the particular judgment that each soul faces at the moment of death, as a preparation for the final judgment. The "loss" that such imperfect Christian souls will "suffer," beginning at their particular judgment, is penitential sorrow mixed with ardent longing for God, as the soul is made to realize, in the light of God's judgment, that its earthly service of God and its love for Him were weak, partial, and compromised. Such are the purifying sufferings of the souls in Purgatory.

Notice that these purgatorial sufferings are mentioned by St. Paul as a matter of Divine Judgment and Divine Justice, as well as a matter of purification and salvation. There is a mystery here, indeed. On the one hand, there seems to be an intermediate state after death where souls receive cleansing, purifying punishments after death, to make up their moral debt to God for their imperfect service and half-hearted repentance while on earth (on the order of Divine Justice). And yet at the same time (on the order of Divine Mercy), this purgatorial state also heals and purifies these souls of their remaining spiritual defects, in order to prepare them for the joys of heaven.

Lest we think that this teaching is merely a peculiarity of the Latin-speaking, Western Fathers of the Church, let's look at some quotes from the ancient Fathers of the Greek-speaking East, who state or imply the same thing.

Take, for example, St. Clement of Alexandria (d. 215 AD), who wrote that those who die reconciled to God but without having completed their penance on earth will be "sanctified [by] a fire which is not a consuming fire like the fire of a forge, but an intelligent fire which penetrates the soul and is traversed by it."[22] Elsewhere in the same work he says that "God's righteousness is good, and His goodness is righteous," and that "the punishments cease in the course of the completion of the expiation and purification of each one ...."[23]

In the fourth century, St. Cyril of Jerusalem (d. 386) wrote: "By offering God our supplications for those who have fallen asleep, if they have sinned, we ... offer Christ sacrificed for the sins of all, and so render favorable for them and for us the God who loves man."[24] Notice that we are said by St. Cyril to offer Christ in the Eucharist for the sins of the faithful departed, to render God "favorable"

---

[22] St. Clement of Alexandria, *Stromata*, cited in Salkeld, *Can Catholics and Evangelicals Agree about Purgatory and the Last Judgment?*, p. 39.

[23] St. Clement of Alexandria, *Stromata*, 6:14, cited in Salza, *The Biblical Basis for Purgatory*, p. 150.

[24] St. Cyril of Jerusalem, *Catechetical Lectures* 23.10, *Myst.* 5.

to them, in other words, to obtain the completion of their divine pardon.[25]

In the fifth century, St. John Chrysostom (d. 407) wrote in his *Third Homily*:

> The apostles did not ordain, without good reason, a commemoration of the departed to be made during the celebration of the mysteries; for from it the deceased draw great gain and help. Why should our prayers for them not placate God, when besides the priest, the whole people stand with uplifted hands while the august Victim [that is, Jesus Christ in the Eucharist] is presented on the altar? True, it is offered only for such as departed hence in faith.

According to this saint and Father of the Church, we are to "placate" Divine Justice by offering prayers at Mass for the faithful departed.

Finally, St. Maximus the Confessor (d. 662) wrote in his work *Questions and Doubts*: "Those departing this life not fully perfect must expiate that which is bad in their balance of good and bad as if by fire" (the Greek here literally says, "as if they were being burned").[26]

---

[25] The use of language here by St. Cyril is not the best — for some reason we need to "render favorable" to imperfectly penitent and deceased sinners "the God who loves man." If He loves them, one might ask, why does he need to be rendered favorable to them by our prayers of supplication at the Eucharist? But St. Cyril was not offering here a complete explanation of the relationship between Divine Mercy and Divine Justice, he was just writing in short about the efficacy of prayers for the departed.

[26] See Migne, *PG* 90, 792-793.

Meanwhile, great saints and mystics of the Church have had visions and prophetic revelations about Purgatory which clearly affirm its penal as well as its purifying nature. For example, Jesus said to St. Faustina regarding Purgatory (as recorded in her *Diary*, entry 1226):

> All these souls are greatly loved by Me. They are making retribution to My justice. It is in your power to bring them relief. Draw all the indulgences from the treasury of My Church and offer them on their behalf. Oh, if you only knew the torments they suffer, you would continually offer for them the alms of the spirit and pay off their debt to My justice.

All of this should be evidence enough, from both Scripture and Sacred Tradition, that there is a Purgatory, and that it includes both a "penal" and a "remedial" dimension. In other words, it involves both the clearing of our remaining moral debt to God, and the final healing and sanctification of the soul on its journey into the Heart of Divine Love.

How can both of these things be true at once? Let's dig deeper ....

Purgatory and God's Merciful Love

The Catholic doctrine of Purgatory is inseparable from the Church's understanding of the distinction between the "temporal" and "eternal" punishment that is due to sin. The *Catechism of the Catholic Church* explains this distinction in entry 1472:

> To understand this doctrine and practice of the Church, it is necessary to understand that sin has a double consequence. Grave sin deprives us of communion

with God and therefore makes us incapable of eternal life, the privation of which is called the "eternal punishment" of sin [in other words, eternal loss or damnation]. On the other hand, every sin, even venial sin, entails an unhealthy attachment to creatures, which must be purified either here on earth or after death in the state called Purgatory. This purification frees one from what is called the "temporal punishment" of sin. These two punishments must not be conceived as a kind of vengeance inflicted by God from without, but as following from the very nature of sin. A conversion which proceeds from fervent charity can attain the complete purification of the sinner in such a way that no punishment remains.

Scripture is replete with examples of the Lord leaving a temporal punishment for sin in place even after someone has attained a measure of repentance and the remission of their sins. In his book *The Salvation Controversy*, James Akin gives some clear examples from the Old Testament, including the following:

> When he forgave [King] David for his sin concerning Uriah, [God] still left David the temporal punishment of having his infant son die and having the sword pass through his house (2 Sam 12:13ff). Similarly, when Moses struck the rock a second time, God forgave him (for Moses was obviously one of the saved, as his appearance on the Mount of Transfiguration illustrates), though he still suffered the temporal penalty of not being allowed to go into the Promised Land (Num 20:12).[27]

---

[27] James Akin, *The Salvation Controversy* (San Diego: Catholic Answers, 2001), p.44.

We find this same distinction between temporal and eternal punishment for sin on display in the New Testament. John Salza provides an excellent example for us from St. Paul's First Epistle to the Corinthians:

> In the New Testament, we see how the Corinthians sinned grievously by receiving the Eucharist unworthily. Paul warned them that receiving the body and blood of Christ in mortal sin would result in eternal punishment when he declared, "Whoever, therefore, eats the bread or drinks the cup of the Lord in an unworthy manner will be guilty of profaning the body and blood of the Lord"; "For anyone who eats and drinks without discerning the body eats and drinks judgment upon himself." [I Cor 11:27, 30]
>
> However, Paul also told the Corinthians that because of their sacrilege they were also suffering temporal punishments of weakness and illness: "That is why many of you are weak and ill, and some have died" (I Cor 11:30). Because the Corinthians abused the flesh of Christ in the Eucharist, God punished their own flesh with sickness and death. This is another example of God's desire to restore the equality of justice between Himself and His creatures."[28]

This distinction between the temporal and eternal penalty for sin also lay behind the penitential system practiced by the early Church. Jesus had promised his apostles: "If you forgive the sins of any, they are forgiven; if you retain the sins of any, they are retained" (Jn 20:23). In the first few centuries of the Church, this meant that when Christians committed grave sins after their baptism, they would have to confess those sins publicly, in the presence of their

---

[28] Salza, *The Biblical Basis for Purgatory*, p. 60-61.

bishop (a successor of the apostles) and before the entire Christian community (I guess we can all be grateful that Irish monks propagated private confession to a priest in the early Middle Ages, and that this became the norm in the Catholic Church thereafter)!

The bishop would only agree to pronounce the public absolution of sinners after they had undergone a period of penance, usually in the form of so many days, months, or years of exclusion from Holy Communion, as well as fasting, and the wearing of penitential clothing ("sackcloth and ashes"). This penance was designed to deepen their contrition and remit their remaining moral debt to God, and it could be shortened by the bishop, or removed completely, on evidence of true, deep, and lasting contrition by the sinner. Once the absolution was finally given by the bishop, no temporal, moral debt to God and His Church for those sins was considered owing any longer.

In later centuries, with the spread of the tradition of private confession to a priest (who is a delegate of the bishop in this regard), the necessary penance or "satisfaction" for sins was projected into the future, so that one either had to complete the purgation of one's soul by accomplishing (with a proper, penitential intention) the penances assigned by the priest, or complete that purification beyond death in Purgatory.

The last sentence of Catechism, entry 1472 (quoted above) is especially important. It talks about the possibility of a deep "conversion" from sin that "proceeds from a fervent charity," thereby resulting in the "complete purification of the sinner in such a way that no punishment [temporal or eternal] would remain." Saint Therese of Lisieux, the Little Flower (1873-1897), discerned this same connection between the spiritual pain of authentic repentance, informed by love of Christ, and the remission of temporal punishment due to sin. Her sister Celine recalled:

> Soeur Therese often repeated to me that the justice of God is satisfied with very little when love is the motive of our reparation; even then He mitigates, to an excessive degree, the *temporal* punishment due to sin, for He is gentleness itself.

> "I have frequently noticed," she confided to me, "that after I have committed a fault, even a slight one, my soul experiences a certain sadness or uneasiness for some little time. Then I tell myself, 'Now, little one, this is the price you must pay for your fault,' and so I patiently bear with the trial until the little debt is paid.

> According to her understanding of the virtue of hope, that was the extent of satisfaction required by Divine Justice for those who are humble and who abandon themselves to God in love. She could not believe such souls would have to go to Purgatory. She thought, rather, that at the moment of death their Father in heaven, because of their confidence, would kindle in their souls as they realized their misery an attitude of perfect contrition, and that in this way their entire debt should be cancelled.[29]

---

[29] Sister Genevieve of the Holy Face (Celine Martin), *My Sister St. Therese* (Rockford, ILL: TAN Books, 1959), p. 61-62. Unfortunately, John Salza in *The Biblical Basis for Purgatory* overlooks this connection between the demands of Divine Justice and internal contrition and purification of the soul: "If God's justice demands that sin be punished, it follows that one who dies with contrition for his sins but before satisfying the full punishment for them will suffer the remaining punishment in

As previously discussed, this explains why Jesus could say to the penitent thief crucified alongside Him on Calvary: "Truly I say to you, today you shall be with me in paradise" (Lk 23:43). The good thief evidently had attained such a true faith in Christ, and such complete repentance for sin (see his words in Lk 23:40-42) that there was no longer any need for temporal punishment or purification in the next life. His purifying penance consisted in his earthly suffering and death alongside Jesus, which brought him to a spiritual state of authentic repentance, faith and love.

Moreover, *Catechism* entry 1472 implies that although there is indeed a penal or judicial aspect of the doctrine of Purgatory, there is no such thing as a solely punitive response by God to human sin. Rather, all of God's acts of justice also express His merciful love, and serve His merciful purposes. In other words, for those who die in a state of grace, but imperfect in repentant faith and love, *the doctrine of Purgatory is an expression of Divine Justice in the service of Divine Mercy.* John Salza sums up this holy mystery for us:

> [T]he doctrine of purgatory is in fact one of the most merciful and consoling doctrines that Scripture teaches. God purifies us from our defects precisely because of

---

the afterlife" (p.16). The point that both *Catechism* 1472, and St. Therese seem to be making, however, is that the purifying inner pain of grace-assisted, profound and perfect contrition for sin, united by faith and love with the Cross of Christ, already satisfies the demands of Divine Justice, and sanctifies the soul at the same time. In I Kings 21:29, for example, King Ahab's repentance for his sins, expressed and deepened by his acts of penance, reduced the punishments that he and his kingdom otherwise would have suffered from God's justice.

His mercy. God refines His children in the fire of His love so that they can fully attain the joys of heaven. ...

In Purgatory God purifies the soul of its imperfections through the fire of His divine justice. During this finite but painful process, the soul is purged of its evil inclinations and makes final satisfaction to God for its sins. After the purification is complete, God admits the soul into heaven where it enjoys the Beatific Vision for all eternity.[30]

As we saw in the previous chapter of this book, the Catholic tradition teaches that Good Friday manifests both the merciful love and the justice of God, for Christ makes "compensation" for our sins on the Cross, paying the penalty for them in our place, and He does so on our behalf, precisely because we were helpless and incapable of making any such offering ourselves. Similarly, as we shall see in the next chapter, when the Eternal Judge condemns a cold-hearted, unrepentant soul to everlasting damnation, it is certainly an act of Divine Justice (Rom 12:19: "Vengeance is mine, I will repay, says the Lord."), but it is also an act of Divine Mercy. As Fr. Benedict Groeschel, CFR, wrote in his book *Healing the Original Wound*:

Hell is a place where those who have turned away from God forever hide from Him. ... Hell is the chosen hiding place of those who look into the loving eyes of God and say no. ... Those who have spent their lives running from God are least miserable in hell, not most miserable.[31]

---

[30] Salza, *The Biblical Basis For Purgatory*, p.10-11 and 9.
[31] Benedict Groeschel, CFR, *Healing the Original Wound* (Ann Arbor: Servant Publications, 1993), p. 220.

More on this in the chapter to come.

In a similar way, the doctrine of Purgatory manifests our Savior's justice, and at the same time His merciful love for us. Those who die in a state of weak love for Christ and weak faith in Him, and who therefore have attained only a half-hearted and partial repentance for their sins, are just not ready for the selfless love and adoration of God that is involved in joyful communion with Him in Heaven. Besides, such souls remain, to some extent, in a state of moral debt to God, because the benefits of Christ's sacrificial death cannot fully apply to those only partially penitent. What, then, can our merciful Savior do for these souls? To cure them of their spiritual defects, pulling them away from their disordered attachments to creatures and from their own pride, is inevitably very painful, just as pulling an infected tooth inevitably involves temporary pain. At the same time, the pain involved in this healing process is perfectly just: it clears their debt to Divine Justice for their half-hearted discipleship and weak repentance. As their spiritual healing process advances, the sufferings of these souls in Purgatory are united more and more to the Cross of Christ, through faith and love, and they therefore partake more and more of its benefits.[32] In

---

[32] Human suffering on its own does not remove the temporal punishment due to sin. In fact, in this life some people grow even more bitter and rebellious against God when suffering befalls them. This only adds new moral debt: more temporal and even eternal punishment due for sin. It is only the sufferings of a soul in a state of grace, offered up (or at least accepted and endured) in repentant faith and love for Christ that are thereby united to the redemptive value of His Cross, and on that basis have expiatory value on the scales of Divine Justice. Such are the

short, the merciful Jesus purifies these souls by applying to them a form of *punishment* that actually *heals* them!

Notice also that this fits perfectly with what the apostles taught about the potentially purifying effects of suffering in this present life. Saint Peter tells us in I Pet 4:1-2, for example, that suffering can be used by God to promote our sanctification. Saint Paul taught in Rom 8:17 that suffering with Christ is actually a pre-requisite for sharing in His eternal glory (cf. Phil 3:10-11 and Heb 12:5).[33]

Of course, as St. Therese of Lisieux saw, those who attain true and perfect contrition in this earthly life, or at the time of death — in other words, those who attain deep

---

sufferings of devout souls on earth, and the sufferings accepted out of love for Jesus Christ by the souls in in Purgatory.

[33] Some Evangelical Christian Scripture commentators suggest that there is no need for anyone to pay off any temporal punishment for sin after death, because all human beings suffer that punishment to a sufficient degree simply by dying, as St. Paul says in Rom 6:23: "the wages of sin is death." But the context of St. Paul's words here in Rom 6:20-23 makes it clear that by "death" in that passage he meant far more than just physical death. As in Rom 5:12-21, "death" for St. Paul includes both bodily and spiritual death from sin, just as "eternal life" for St. Paul means an everlasting fullness of life, both physical and spiritual. That is why he writes in Rom 6:22-23: "But now that you have been set free from sin and have become slaves of God, the return you get is sanctification and its end, eternal life. For the wages of sin is death, but the free gift of God is eternal life in Christ Jesus our Lord." Also, bodily death all by itself would not pay even the temporal "the wages of sin" for anyone unless it was accompanied by deep repentance and faith out of love for Jesus Christ, See footnote 32, above.

penitence for their sins out of true love for God and true faith in Him — are already sufficiently purified. Christ's sacrifice on the Cross can thereby cover all the debt to Divine Justice due for their sins, both temporal and eternal, and at the same time they are filled to overflowing with His grace. They go directly to heaven upon their death. But for the rest of us, our repentance is usually motivated more by fear of the consequences of our sins and disgust at ourselves, than by fervent charity for God and our neighbors. We are not so much concerned that we have let Him down, who infinitely loved us, and we have not yet put our whole trust in Him. We still need to let go of our improper pride, and our disordered, worldly attachments: a "letting-go" and healing process that can be completed beyond death in Purgatory, by the merciful love of God. Brett Salkeld put it well: "Purgatory can be understood as an affirmation of the biblical promise 'that the one who began a good work among you will bring it to completion by the day of Jesus Christ' (Phil 1:6) even if we do not see this good work completed by the time of biological death."[34]

The Spiritual Pain of Purgatory: Longing for God

Catholics and those from other Christian traditions have sometimes "fallen out" with each other on the nature of purgatorial pain. What does this divine surgery on the soul really involve? Is it a real "fire" that somehow heals? Father Kenneth Baker, SJ, reflected on this aspect of the mystery of Purgatory in volume three of his *Fundamentals of Catholicism*:

---

[34] Salkeld, *Can Catholics and Evangelicals Agree about Purgatory and the Last Judgment*, p.12.

We are not certain about the nature of the punishment of purgatory. The Church does not teach dogmatically that it is a "physical fire," even though many preachers and some catechisms speak of "the fires of purgatory." The official declarations of the Councils speak only of purifying punishments, not purifying fire. Whatever it is, it is painful.[35]

We need to go beyond Fr. Baker's reflections here, however, and say that this "fire" cannot *literally* be "physical" fire because the souls in Purgatory were separated from their bodies at death, and will not receive new, heavenly bodies until the final Judgment Day.[36] Moreover, the Church has never definitively taught that the experience of the "fires" of Purgatory is akin to the experience of the souls of the damned, suffering in the fires of hell — as if Purgatory is simply a temporary experience of hell. Indeed, *Catechism* 1031 seems to dispel that notion when it states that in Purgatory, "this final

---

[35] Baker, *Fundamentals of Catholicism*, volume three (San Francisco: Ignatius Press, 1983), p. 375-376.

[36] This puts a question mark over some of the physical evidence and accompanying testimonials collected and on display in the *Piccolo Museo del Purgatorio* (Little Museum of Purgatory) at the Church of the Sacred Heart of Refuge in Rome. This material is discussed and analyzed in Gerard J.M. Van Den Aardweg, *Hungry Souls: Supernatural Visits, Messages, and Warnings from Purgatory.* It includes such things as scorch marks on books, cloths and tables allegedly touched by the hands of the burning flesh of these suffering souls. The fact that only in one case does any physical evidence and testimonial come from the life and witness of a saint, blessed, or venerable soul of the Church also provides some reason for doubt.

purification of the elect ... is entirely different from the punishment of the damned."

It is sometimes argued that God could cause disembodied souls to be afflicted with a "pain of sense" just as excruciating as that of burning alive simply by permitting those souls to experience the precise equivalent of the sensory impression of burning, without using physical fire. No doubt He could do this, but it brings up another issue. The idea that God would cause souls to experience a pain of sense as horrifying as burning alive, and not allow them to lapse into unconsciousness from shock after 20 seconds or so (which is what would happen to someone engulfed in flames in this life), but force them to remain fully aware and endure it in Purgatory for an extended period of time — all this seems grossly *unjust and disproportionate*, given that the souls upon whom God would be inflicting this extreme punishment would be souls in a state of grace: despite their imperfections, they are fundamentally oriented to His love. Thankfully, the Church has never definitively taught that the fires of Purgatory are the equivalent in conscious sensation of the experience of burning alive by physical fire.

We do not need to take the biblical and traditional language about purgatorial flames *literally*, therefore, but we do need to take such language *seriously*. This metaphor of "fire" must refer to some kind of burning *spiritual* pain. Saint Gregory of Nyssa once wrote in his *Sermon about the Dead* that a human being "is not able to partake of divinity until he has been purged of the filthy contagion in his soul by the purifying fire."[37]

---

[37] Saint Gregory of Nyssa, *Sermon about the Dead*, cited in Salza, *The Biblical Basis for Purgatory*, p. 161.

Thus, the fires of Purgatory must be painful, but necessary to our spiritual healing, and to the clearing of any remaining moral debt to God's justice for our sins. Saint Theresa of Avila once wrote:

> The pain of loss, or the privation of the sight of God, exceeds all the most excruciating [spiritual] sufferings we can imagine, because the souls urged on towards God as to the center of their aspiration, are continually repulsed by His justice. Picture to yourself a shipwrecked mariner who, after having battled with the waves, comes at last within the reach of the shore, only to find himself constantly thrust back by an invisible hand.[38]

In fact, many Catholic saints have had private revelations, sometimes in the form of visions, about the nature of the spiritual surgery that souls undergo in Purgatory. Although such testimony is not the equivalent of definitive teaching by the Church's Magisterium, it would be rash and imprudent to contradict the concurrent testimony of the saints, given that they were full to overflowing with the Holy Spirit, the Spirit of Truth and Love. We can be sure that the reason God unveiled this mystery to His saints was not simply to frighten them, or their readers about the nature of Purgatory, but to move us with compassion for the souls undergoing purification there, and to urge us all to come to their aid. Saint Stanislaus Papczynski (d. 1701), founder of the Congregation of Marian Fathers of the Immaculate Conception, received several visions of the state of the souls in Purgatory, and as a result he exhorted

---

[38] Saint Theresa of Avila, *Interior Castle*, part 6, chapter 11.

his companions: "Pray brethren, for the souls in Purgatory, for they suffer unbearably."[39]

Many saints of the Church testify that the Lord revealed to them the deepest suffering of the souls in *Purgatory: longing for union with God*. Father Kenneth Baker, SJ, sums up this testimony:

> The souls in Purgatory ... know for certain that they are saved; in this they rejoice. But since they need cleansing they are separated from God for a time. This separation is most painful to them, since their whole being longs to be united with God.[40]

Perhaps the saint who contemplated this mystery in greatest depth — the mystery of the pain of spiritual longing of the souls in Purgatory — was St. Catherine of Genoa (d. 1510 AD). In her book *The Spiritual Dialogue* she wrote:

> God inspires the soul in purgatory with so ardent a movement of devoted love that it would be sufficient to annihilate her were she not immortal. Illumined and inflamed by pure charity, the more she loves God, the more she detests the least stain of sin that displeases Him, the least hindrance that prevents her union with Him.... [She is] impelled by the impetuosity of the love which exists between God and herself, in order that she might be the sooner delivered from all that separates her from her sovereign God.[41]

---

[39] Cited in Tassone, *Praying with the Saints for the Holy Souls in Purgatory*, p. 82.
[40] Baker, *Fundamentals of Catholicism*, vol. 3, p. 375.
[41] Saint Catherine of Genoa, *The Spiritual Dialogue*.

In the 20th century, we find a similar teaching in a classic theological meditation on the afterlife by Fr. J.P. Arendzen, titled *Purgatory and Heaven*. Commenting on St. Catherine's perspective, he remarks:

> The state of the Holy Souls can be summed up in these words: an intense, unsatisfied desire to see God. ... The flames of Purgatory may be metaphorical, but they are at least a metaphor for a reality which far exceeds mere bodily pain. Even on earth an unsatisfied desire may become an acute mental pain, a consuming anguish .... On earth we find a respite in merciful sleep, but in purgatory there is an incessant and sleepless yearning thought: God! ... [God] calls the soul to Himself, yet the soul cannot yet come. Hearing this call, it answers with a flaming desire to leap forward, and yet must remain away, till the very vehemence and duration of its holy desires have undone the havoc which sin had wrought.[42]

This same understanding of the suffering of the souls in Purgatory was revealed to St. Faustina as well, the great Apostle of Divine Mercy. She recorded in her *Diary*:

> I saw my Guardian angel who ordered me to follow him. In a moment I was in a misty place full of fire in which there was a great crowd of suffering souls. They were praying fervently, but to no avail, for themselves; only we can come to their aid. The flames which were burning them did not reach me at all. My Guardian Angel did not leave me for an instant. I asked these souls what their greatest suffering was. *They answered me*

---

[42] J.P. Arendzen, D.D., *Purgatory and Heaven* (Charlotte, NC: TAN books, 2012 edition), p. 19-25.

in one voice that their greatest torment was longing for God. (*Diary*, entry 20)

The "flames" of Purgatory mentioned here may be a symbolic way of expressing the painful desire of these holy souls for God. The "fire" of longing for God in their hearts purifies them of any remaining attachment to sin. It prepares them for final union with Christ in heaven. Moreover, all this happens within them by the power of the Holy Spirit, who is described in the New Testament as the "fire" that came down upon the Church at Pentecost, the same spiritual fire that St. John of the Cross once referred to as "The Living Flame of Love." Pope Benedict XVI echoed this same connection between the spiritual fire of the Spirit of Christ and the flames of Purgatory when he wrote in his encyclical letter *Spe Salvi* (Saved in Hope, 2007):

> Some recent theologians are of the opinion that the fire which both burns and saves is Christ himself, the Judge and Savior. ... His gaze, the touch of his heart heals us through an undeniably painful transformation "as through fire." But it is a blessed pain, in which the holy power of his love sears through us like a flame, enabling us to become totally ourselves and thus totally of God. (section 47)

Brett Salkeld offers his own translation of a passage from the writings of St. Catherine of Genoa, a passage that expresses this same point with tremendous beauty:

> The soul is like gold, which, the more it is fired, the more it becomes pure and the more its imperfections are obliterated. Fire works this same way on all material things. The soul, however, cannot be annihilated in God, but is purified more and more in itself, so that

dying to itself it rests purely in   God. Gold, when it is purified to 24 carats, will no longer be consumed by the fire to which it is drawn, because the fire cannot consume anything that is not imperfection. In the same way the divine fire works on the soul .... [A]fter the soul is purified to 24 carats, it is rendered immutable because there remains nothing left that can be consumed. The soul, having been purified in this way and being held, still in the fire, feels no longer any pain. On the contrary, it remains in the fire of divine love for all eternity, containing in itself nothing contrary to that love.[43]

All this is important because it helps dispel a popular misunderstanding. Purgatory is not a geographically located "place" in which the Holy Souls are suffering from physical flames and the temporary "absence" of God: rather, it is a state or condition — in a purely spiritual dimension of existence, we might say — in which their hearts are being immersed and purified in the refiner's fire of God's love, and by His Holy Spirit, more and more.[44]

---

[43] Caterina da Genova, *Trattato del Purgatorio* Palermo: Sellerio editore, 2004), p. 42-43 cited and translated in Salkeld, *Can Catholics and Evangelicals Agree About Purgatory and the Last Judgment?*, p. 26-27.

[44] This seems to be what Pope St. John Paul II meant when he spoke about Purgatory in his Wednesday Audience Address on August 4th, 1999, remarks that were considered controversial at the time. Purgatory is not a place under the earth somewhere, but a spiritual dimension of existence, in the nearer presence of God's love:

Purification must be complete, and this is precisely what is meant by the Church's teaching on *purgatory*.   The   term does not indicate a place, but a condition of existence. Those who, after death, exist in a state of purification are already in

How We Can Help the Souls in Purgatory

From the concurrent testimony of these saints, popes, and theologians, it seems clear that God did not unveil this mystery to the Church primarily to frighten us about the fires of Purgatory.[45] Rather, He revealed these mysteries to the Church in order to fill us with hope, that even if our loved ones died with just a tiny spark of true faith and love in their hearts, the God of mercy can fan that spark into flame, and find a way home to Heaven for them. Moreover, He revealed the state of the suffering souls in Purgatory to us to fill us with *compassion* for them, so that we would be moved to come to their aid.

The Catholic Church teaches that to help the souls suffering in Purgatory by prayer and other good works is an act of sublime charity. As the *Catechism of the Catholic Church* tells us in entry 1032, the Church "commends almsgiving, indulgences and works of penance undertaken on behalf of the dead," and this *Catechism* passage quotes St. John Chrysostom in this regard as well:

> Let us help and commemorate them. If Job's sons were purified by their father's sacrifice, why would we doubt that our offerings for the dead bring them some

---

the love of Christ who removes from them the remnants of imperfection. (no. 5)

[45] The unfortunate effect of the way the testimony of many saints and blessed is reported and arranged in the book by F.X. Schouppe, S.J., *Purgatory Explained* (Rockford, IL: TAN books, 1989, originally published in 1893).

consolation? Let us not hesitate to help those who have died, and to offer our prayers for them.

According to St. Augustine, "One of the holiest works, one of the best exercises of piety that we can practice in this world, is to offer sacrifices, alms, and prayers for the dead" (Homily 16). This is so because the souls in Purgatory, some of whom suffer greatly and for a prolonged period, cannot help themselves to shorten their time of purification. In that sense their time for prayer for themselves, and active striving for virtue is over — only the faithful on earth can come to their aid.

Nothing could be easier for us than to include this daily prayer intention as part of our spiritual life. Here is a simple way to do so: Every time you suffer some cross or misfortune, offer it up to our merciful Savior in words borrowed from the traditional Morning Offering: "Merciful Jesus, I offer you this cross in union with the Holy Sacrifice of the Mass throughout the world, for all the intentions you had on Your Heart in Your agony and passion, especially for the conversion of sinners, in reparation for my own sins, for the relief of the souls suffering in Purgatory, and for Holy Father's intentions for this month." Another way is to pray at every Mass for the souls suffering in Purgatory, especially for those suffering the longest purification, and who are most forgotten by their friends and relations on earth. Saint Faustina provides us with a prayer we can say for the Holy Souls at any time:

Eternal Father, turn Your merciful gaze upon the souls suffering in purgatory, who are enfolded in the Most Compassionate Heart of Jesus. I beg You, by the sorrowful Passion of Jesus Your Son, and by all the bitterness with which His most sacred Soul was flooded, manifest Your mercy to the souls who are under Your just scrutiny. Look upon them in no other way than through the wounds of Jesus, Your dearly beloved Son; for we firmly believe that there is no limit to Your goodness and compassion. (*Diary*, 1227)

The Church and the saints also encourage us to offer indulgences for the souls suffering in Purgatory.

What is an Indulgence? An indulgence is a way the Church assures us that certain pious acts, when performed by us with the assistance of the Holy Spirit, can unite us in a supreme way with the superabundant merits of Christ's life and death, enabling us in turn to merit graces for ourselves and others. Christ's gift of indulgences to us through His Church is meant to be a personal experience of his solidarity with us, and with all the saints, in love and grace.

Sadly, the Catholic Church sometimes took advantage of this good intention by the faithful. In the Middle Ages especially, the clergy and religious extracted money from the laity to obtain "indulgences" for their loved ones in Purgatory, and encouraged the wealthy to endow Church projects in return for prayers and masses to be said on an ongoing basis for their salvation. These corruptions were rectified, however, back in the 16th century at the time of the Protestant Reformation, when Pope St. Pius V declared that indulgences should never be sold for money, and Pope Adrian VI insisted that a work of piety for which an indulgence has been offered by the Church is of little benefit to anyone in Purgatory without the proper dispositions of penitence, faith and love in the hearts of those who perform that pious work.[46]

---

[46] It is also worth noting, as Salkeld does, that in 997 AD, Odilo, the abbot of Cluny in France, was the first to introduce the Feast of All Souls "to counter the concern that the rich may have more

The Church distinguishes between partial and plenary indulgences. A plenary indulgence removes all of the temporal punishment due to sin, while a partial indulgence removes only part of that debt. The Church makes this distinction between plenary and partial indulgences because some of our good acts have the potential to be life-changing acts of conversion (if undertaken with the help of the Holy Spirit, and with true love for God and faithful repentance for sin), while other good acts represent smaller, but still very important steps on the journey to deeper conversion of heart. As we unite our acts and efforts to the grace and merits of Jesus and the works and merits of the saints, the Church calls us to persevere day by day in our path to holiness.[47]

Both forms of indulgence are gifts of God's transforming love, and both forms meet the demands of Divine Justice at the same time. We can obtain them for ourselves or for the sake of the faithful departed, who are completing their final purification in Purgatory. We can offer up an indulgenced work of penance, charity or piety on behalf of a particular soul, but it is always up to God in the end to determine to whom it will be applied (after all, unknown to

---

access to aid while in purgatory due to their ability to endow churches or monasteries with funds to procure Masses for their souls" (p. 45).

[47] The preceding paragraphs on the theology of indulgences are adapted in part from a brief tract by Fr. John Horgan of the Archdiocese of Vancouver, quoted with permission in the online document "Understanding Divine Mercy Sunday" at https://www.thedivinemercy.org/assets/pdf/jpii/UnderstandDM.pdf.

us, the person for whom we offer up an indulgence may already be out of Purgatory, and no longer in need of it).

Father Arendzen sums up what we can hope for from all our works of charity and piety on behalf of the Holy Souls:

> When a man prays for the souls in purgatory, though his prayer may not obtain the immediate total release of any of them, he knows that he directly comforts them in some measure, that he brightens the twilight of their prison-house, that someone at least in his innermost being feels the happy results of his prayer.
> ...
> God, for our sakes by some creative action of His omnipotence, speeds up and intensifies the energies of that soul. He fills it with greater energy in suffering, in desiring, in reaching out to God, that its task may be the sooner done.[48]

The Saints on the Joys of Purgatory

Let us also not forget also the profound joy of the souls in Purgatory. Theirs is not a state of unmitigated longing and penitential sorrow. Rather, according to Catholic Tradition, at the moment of its particular judgment, and at the start of the soul's journey through Purgatory, each one is given a vision of Jesus Himself, and it is reasonable to assume that this vision comforts and sustains them through all the purifying sufferings they must undergo. Father Frederick Faber once wrote:

> [T]he soul goes into Purgatory with its eyes fascinated and its spirit sweetly tranquilized by the face of Jesus, its first sight of the Sacred Humanity, at the Particular

---

[48] Arendzen, *Purgatory and Heaven*, p. 38, 37.

Judgment which it has undergone. That vision abides with it still, and beautifies the uneven terrors of its prison as if with perpetual silvery showers of moonlight which seem to fall from our Saviour's loving eyes. In the sea of fire it holds fast by that image.[49]

Souls in the state of Purgatory also rejoice in the assurance that their purification will unfailingly lead them to the full and glorious vision in Heaven of their Savior. Saint Catherine of Genoa wrote: "I do not believe that it is possible to find a contentment to compare with that of the souls in purgatory, unless it be the contentment of the Saints in Paradise."[50] St. Francis De Sales (d. 1622) once wrote that just as the pains of Purgatory are severe, so the interior satisfaction and bliss enjoyed by the souls there must surpass anything we can imagine. How wonderful it must be for the suffering souls when they feel themselves being spiritually healed: gradually freed from their remaining attachments to sin and their moral debt to God's justice, and gradually drawing nearer and nearer to the joyful vision of the Blessed Trinity![51]

---

[49] Fr. Frederick William Faber, *Purgatory* (Charlotte, NC: TAN Books, 2002, reprint of 1854 edition), p. 18.

[50] Cited in Tassone, *Praying with the Saints for the Holy Souls in Purgatory*, p. 84.

[51] Catholic theologian Michael Schmaus defined the soul's journey through Purgatory precisely in terms of this ever deeper liberation from the prison of the self:

> The soul's purification consists precisely in this process: the human "I' is gradually pervaded by the divine love, with the effect that the person is increasingly freed of imprisonment within himself. He likewise becomes more capable of the divine self-communication. (*Dogma, 6: Justification and the Last Things*. Kansas City: Sheed and Ward, 1977, p. 244)

Let's close this exploration of the truth about Purgatory with two quotations, statements that probably capture the heart of this doctrine as well as human words can express it.

First, many years ago Fr. Seraphim Michalenko, MIC, wrote the following meditation which holds together in a few paragraphs the paradox of merciful love and justice, suffering and joy, all wrapped up in the great mystery of Purgatory:

> To whatever extent we become conscious, during our earthly lives, of our inability to rid ourselves completely of whatever blocks us from intimate union with God, we feel [spiritual] pain. We experience a taste of "Purgatory," recognizing how perfectly God loves us, and how imperfectly we love Him in return.
>
> In Purgatory this pain is heightened, lifted in a sense to infinity, by the Divine Light that reveals to us at once the infinity and purity of Divine Love, and the full extent of our inordinate self-love.
>
> We are filled with longing for God, whom we now, more than ever before, realize is the only One who can bring us to the fullness of joy. And we suffer the pain of separation from the object of our longing, knowing that it is a separation caused by our own self-centeredness.
>
> But although this is a very real and intense form of suffering, it yet carries with it a character of "sweetness and hope" which we can call purgatorial joy! This joy of souls is the result of having trustingly handed themselves over to God and accepted the purification that arises from their love and longing as their misery truly meets His mercy.

Purgatory is our meeting with Christ who loves us, and of our loving acceptance of His pardoning love. It is our passage to holiness. It is not yet heaven, but it is a definite way to it, since the love of God underlies the purifying suffering of souls. ... The souls in Purgatory already definitely belong to God and nothing can separate them from Him.

The second quote certainly had nothing to do with Purgatory when it was first written, because it was penned by an 18th century Protestant hymn writer, Charles Wesley. Nevertheless, it sums up beautifully the heart's longing of all souls in the state of purgation — both in this life, and the life to come:

Finish then Thy new creation
Pure and spotless let us be;
Let us see Thy great salvation,
Perfectly restored in Thee;

Changed from glory into glory
Till in heaven we take our place,
Till we cast our crowns before Thee
Lost in wonder, love and praise.

Chapter Four
If God is so Merciful, Why is there a Hell?

The most uncomfortable truth of all regarding Divine Justice, of course, is the traditional doctrine of damnation: the doctrine that God ultimately consigns some people to everlasting hell-fire. That Catholics generally ignore this doctrine is manifestly obvious (for example, when was the last time you heard a Sunday homily on this topic?). In fact, today some Catholic theologians and Scripture scholars have their doubts that anyone at all will end up eternally lost.

What Did Jesus Teach about Hell?

Scholars of the New Testament, for example, have long noticed that in St. Luke's Gospel, traditionally called "the Gospel of Mercy," Jesus makes only scant, explicit reference to anyone ending up in hell. At first glance, the comparison with the other gospels is striking. If you look in the concordance at the back of the Ignatius Catholic Study Bible New Testament, for example, you will find seven passages listed that explicitly mention "hell" from the Gospel According to St. Matthew, three from St. Mark's Gospel, but only one from St. Luke. In Luke 12: 4-5, Jesus says:

> I tell you, my friends, do not fear those who kill the body, and after that have no more they can do. But I will warn you whom to fear; fear him who after he has killed, has power to cast into hell [the word translated as "hell" here is *gehenna*[1]]; yes, I tell you, fear him.

---

[1] According to Easton's Bible Dictionary, "*Gehenna* was a deep, narrow glen to the south of Jerusalem, where the idolatrous Jews offered their children in sacrifice to Molech (2 Chronicles 28:3; 33:6; Jeremiah 7:31; 19:2-6). This valley afterwards became the common receptacle for all the refuse of the city. Here the dead bodies of

This is the sole explicit reference to hell in Luke — although certainly a stark and sobering one.

There are no explicit mentions of hell listed at all from St. John's Gospel, but that does not mean that the notion of "hell" is absent from this Gospel altogether. In John 5:28-29, for example, Jesus teaches about final judgment and the real danger of eternal loss in the words: "The hour is coming when all who are in the tombs will hear his voice and come forth, those who have done good, to the resurrection of life, and those who have done evil, to the resurrection and judgment." In addition, in John 17 when Jesus prays for his disciples on the night before His arrest, He mentions that "none of them is lost but the son of perdition, that the Scripture might be fulfilled" (Jn 17:12, cf. Ps 13:18, Acts 1:20). This passage clearly refers to Judas Iscariot, who would betray Him, and yet it is not entirely clear that Jesus is predicting here that Judas will be *eternally* lost (for He uses the present tense:

---

animals and of criminals, and all kinds of filth, were cast and consumed by fire kept always burning. It thus in process of time became the image of the place of everlasting destruction. In this sense it is used by our Lord in Matthew 5:22 Matthew 5:29 Matthew 5:30 ; 10:28 ; 18:9 ; Matthew 23:15 Matthew 23:33 ; Mark 9:43 Mark 9:45 Mark 9:47 ; Luke 12:5." However, in the *Mishnah*, a collection of rabbinical teachings in the 2nd century AD, *Gehenna* was also used to describe a place of temporary punishment for sin, akin to the Catholic understanding of Purgatory. Some of the early Fathers of the Church believed that Jesus used the word in this latter sense in Matthew 5 and 18, given the context of his remarks (see, for example, 5:26 and 18:34). However, in some places our Lord uses the word in a way that clearly implies the eternity of punishment in *Gehenna* (see MT 18:8-9; 23:13-15; Mk 9;43-48; Lk 12: 4-12). It seems that the word could be used in both ways.

"is lost," that is, "he is a lost soul at the moment"). Couple this saying with Matthew 26:24, however, where Jesus says that it would have been better for his betrayer "if he had never been born," and the gospels do seem to indicate at least the likelihood that Judas would never make it to the eternal kingdom (After all, how could you say, even hyperbolically, that someone would have been better off if they had never been born if the final destination of their life was to be everlasting joy and splendour in heaven?). In any case, if we widen our gaze at the Johannine literature in the New Testament to include the Book of Revelation, we find several references to the everlasting punishment of the wicked (we shall explore these passages later in this chapter).

In fact, when we look beyond *explicit* statements in Luke's Gospel about hell, we find several *implicit* references worth noting. For example, in Luke 3: 9-17, St. John the Baptist speaks about the "unquenchable fire" that awaits the "chaff," that is, those who do not bear good fruit in their lives, while the "wheat" makes it safely into the Lord's eternal granary. Moreover, in Luke 12:9 Jesus warns: "he who denies me before men *will be denied before the angels of God*" — evidently a reference to the Judgment Day — and in 12:10 Jesus mentions a sin against the Holy Spirit that never can be forgiven. In Luke 13:27-28, in the Parable of the Narrow Door, Jesus says, "Depart from me, all you workers of iniquity. There you will weep and gnash your teeth, when you see Abraham, and Isaac, and Jacob, and all the prophets in the kingdom of God, *and you yourselves thrust out.*" So it appears that the unrepentant workers of iniquity will be denied access to the heavenly kingdom. Finally, in the Parable of the Rich Man and Lazarus, while not (I think) intended by Our Lord to be an entirely realistic portrait of the afterlife as it is now (He names it mythically as "Hades," and, in any case, it describes a state of affairs prior to Christ's death and resurrection), still, Jesus seems to warn here of an inescapable destiny of torment in the next life for those who have been cruel and heartless to the poor (Lk 16:26).

Nevertheless, compared to St. Matthew's Gospel, the doctrine of hell is relegated to the background in Luke and John. They evidently did not see fit to highlight or emphasize our Lord's teachings in this regard as a central part of the gospel message. Thus, we are entitled to ask: why the curious *pianissimo* in Luke and John about the everlasting damnation of the unrepentant enemies of God?

An historian might conclude that St. Luke and St. John did not choose to put Christ's teachings on hell in the foreground because, by and large, they were mostly indistinguishable from the beliefs of most of the Jews of the day (especially among Jewish-Christians of the *diaspora* — that is, outside of Palestine — for whom St. Luke and St. John probably wrote their gospels). Apart from the party of the Sadducees who ran the Temple in Jerusalem, most Jews seem to have believed that there would indeed be a final Judgment Day, that the righteous keepers of God's Law would receive an everlasting reward, while the unrighteous would be sent for everlasting punishment to the "abyss," or "the pit" (sometimes called Tartarus, which was held to be the lowest level of Hades or Sheol, as in Lk 16:22-26), also called an everlasting *Gehenna* (the rubbish pit outside Jerusalem where the garbage fire perpetually burned). As there was nothing distinctively Christian in such beliefs about the afterlife (in fact, even some pagans in the Roman Empire held similar views), there was no reason for St. Luke, or St. John — or Jesus, for that matter — to belabor the point.

Ever since the dawn of the so-called "Enlightenment" in the late 17th- early 18th centuries, however, some Protestant biblical scholars and theologians have wanted to take this matter a bit further. Perhaps the relative silence about hell in the Gospels of St. Luke and St. John not only shows that this doctrine was not of central importance to the early Church (i.e., that it was not high on their list of revealed truths — after all, it is not explicitly mentioned in the Nicene Creed), but also shows that it is not essential to the gospel message at all. Perhaps it is even *dispensable*: maybe we can discard it altogether and still leave the gospel message essentially intact.

Some scholars suggest it was not even considered essential by Jesus Himself. Maybe He just spoke the way He did about hell in order to adapt Himself temporarily to the mythical worldview of his hearers, utilizing mythical themes in order to express truths of much greater importance. Again, perhaps the Parable of the Rich Man and Lazarus, set in mythical Hades, was primarily intended as a warning that God would not stand for anything less than compassion and justice for the poor; it was not primarily intended to teach anything substantial about eternal, final destinies and life after death. Anglican New Testament scholar Marcus Borg put it this way:

> It is possible that Jesus did believe in a final judgment in which some people would go to hell. It is also possible, at least equally so, that the after-life was not a central concern to Jesus, and that he used the language of final judgment to reinforce the importance of acting compassionately. We can imagine the language working this way: You who believe in final judgement — what do you think the basis, the criterion [of that judgement] will be?[2]

In short, some Protestant biblical scholars and theologians today believe that there is only an uncertain basis in the

---

[2] Marcus Borg, *Jesus: the Life, Teachings and Relevance of a Religious Revolutionary* (New York: Harper Collins, 2006), p. 180.

teachings of Jesus for the classical Christian belief that some souls — the wicked and unrepentant — will suffer eternal loss.

Catholic Soft-Universalism

Over the past fifty years or so, Catholic scholars too have been revising their understanding of the doctrine of hell.

A new approach was launched in the Catholic world in 1986 by Hans Urs von Balthasar in his book in German *Dare We Hope "That All Men Be Saved"?*[3] Balthasar was not trying to revive the ancient heresy called "universalism": the belief expressed by a minority of early Christian writers (such as Origen of Alexandria and St. Gregory of Nyssa) that all of humanity eventually will be saved. Rather, Balthasar offered a much more subtle position, a kind of "soft universalism," arguing not that we can be sure that all will be saved in the end, but that we can at least *legitimately hope* that all will be saved, because (so Balthasar claimed) neither Holy Scripture, nor Sacred Tradition, nor human reason rule out either the *possibility*, nor even the *probability* of universal salvation.

Notice carefully what Balthasar is claiming here. It is not just that we can legitimately *desire* that all will be saved. That really goes without saying, for authentic love always seeks and longs for the good of others; certainly, God Himself desires the salvation of all in that sense, according to I Timothy 2:4. But the virtue of "hope" is more than "desire": it is *desire, plus a reasonable assurance that this desire can and will be fulfilled*. Balthasar claims that we do, in fact, have at least some grounds for believing that all will be saved in the end — although not decisive or conclusive grounds.

---

[3] See Hans Urs von Balthasar, *Dare We Hope "That All Men Be Saved"?* (San Francisco: Ignatius Press, 2014 edition).

Moreover, notice that Balthasar does not just argue for the theoretical possibility that all will be saved. He knew very well that such a theoretical possibility would be irrelevant if we still had *overwhelmingly probable* grounds for believing that all will not, in fact, be saved (NB: such overwhelming probability is what philosophers call "moral certainty"— as in the law courts, when the evidence is so strong for someone's guilt that they are found to be guilty "beyond a reasonable doubt"). For example, it is theoretically possible that the sun will not rise tomorrow morning (it might explode in a super-nova overnight) but we could surely cobble together a concurrence of scientific evidence that makes it overwhelmingly probable, true beyond any reasonable doubt whatsoever, that the sun will indeed rise tomorrow. The mere theoretical possibility of the sun not rising tomorrow is so minute that it is not worth bothering about.

So, Balthasar was not just arguing for the bare theoretical *possibility* of universal salvation, but, again, for that possibility bolstered by some reasonable grounds, and therefore some balance of *probability* that the salvation of all will turn out to be the case.

A fairly clear and succinct summary and endorsement of Balthasar's position can be found in Cardinal Walter Kasper's book, *Mercy: The Essence of the Gospel and the Key to the Christian Life* (first German edition, 2013). In Chapter five, section 4, he begins with what appears at first to be a robust defence of the probability that some will suffer eternal loss, based on the reality of human free will:

> Precisely in his mercy, God takes us seriously. He does not want to ambush us mortals or bypass our freedom. Our eternal destiny depends on our decision and our response to the offer of God's love. Love can court the other and

wants to court the other, but it cannot and does not want to force the beloved's response. God's love, therefore, desires to be reciprocated, but people can also ignore or reject it. Because we are created for God's love, its rejection means the self-negation of the human being, and, thereby, his or her total misfortune. Theologically speaking, the rejection of God's love entails the loss of one's eternal beatitude. That proves the seriousness of our freedom. Our life decision is a decision for life or for death.[4]

After this sobering start, however, Kasper moves on to consider Balthasar's position. He notes with approval Balthasar's claim that the Holy Scriptures are actually paradoxical (or at least ambiguous) about life after death.[5] There are passages which seem to support universal salvation, and others which seem to contradict it. Seeking to steer a middle way between what Kasper calls "a cheap optimism" about final salvation, and a "hell-fearing pessimism," Kasper writes:

[In the Bible] we are not actually dealing with … an anticipatory report of what will happen at the end of time. The assertions about universal salvation are statements of hope for all, but they are not assertions about the factual salvation of every individual. Conversely, the assertions about judgment and the statements about hell do not intend to say, about any one individual or about the majority of humankind, that factually they will be subjected to the pains of hell. … Thus, the statements

---

[4] Cardinal Walter Kasper, *Mercy: The Essence of the Gospel and the Key to Christian Life* (New York" Paulist Press, 2014), p. 102-103.
[5] We will discuss Balthasar's claim about Holy Scripture in this regard later in this chapter.

about hell are words of warning, which admonish us to repent. They put hell before our eyes as a real possibility .... [6]

Ultimately, Cardinal Kasper claims, the final destiny of humanity (salvation for all, or only for some) is a mystery that has not been clearly revealed to us. He does not hold as decisive the rational argument that he started with: that some will be lost because God's love is committed to respecting their freedom, including their freedom definitively to reject his love. Instead, Kasper endorses a view expressed by St. Edith Stein that (so Kasper claims) at least *balances* that free will argument. He writes:

> Edith Stein (Sister Theresa of the Cross) attempted to go beyond the mere interplay of divine and human freedom and, as far as that is possible for us, to penetrate God's courtship of the human person and to describe it in depth. She even talks about how God's merciful love *outwits* every human person. Her reflections lead to the theoretical possibility of the salvation of all. Still, the boundary remains: we can hope for the salvation of all, but factually we cannot know that all will be saved.[7]

There is the trendy, contemporary Catholic view in a nutshell: *We can legitimately hope for the salvation of all* — and as we have seen, to "legitimately hope" means more than just to *desire* universal salvation, or hold it as *remotely possible*. For with Kasper, Balthasar and St. Edith Stein, we can find reasons to believe that all will be saved, to give the notion some probability — although, we cannot know *for certain* that all will be saved.

---

[6] Ibid., p. 107.
[7] Ibid., p. 109; italics mine.

The principal popularizer of Balthasar's position in North America has been Bishop Robert Barron, especially in his (in many respects excellent) book titled *Catholicism*, a book we have considered before. He starts out with some helpful clarifications. Barron wrote:

> We human beings can respond to the divine love or we can reject it. We can bask in its light or we can turn from it. The choice is ours. God wants all people to be saved, which is just another way of saying that He wants them all to share His life. But His life is love freely given, and therefore it can be had only in the measure that it is freely returned. "Hell" is a special metaphor for the state of having freely refused this love, having chosen to live outside its ambit.[8]

But then toward the bottom of the same page he begins to wander:

> Though we must accept the possibility of hell (due to the play between divine love and human freedom), we are not committed doctrinally to saying that anyone is actually "in" such a place. We can't see fully to the depths of anyone's heart; only God can. Accordingly, we can't declare with utter certitude that anyone — even Judas, even Hitler — has chosen definitively to lock the door against divine love. Indeed, since the liturgy compels us to pray for all of the dead, and since the law of prayer is the law of belief, we must hold out at least the hope that all people will be saved. Furthermore, since Christ went to the very limits of godforsakeness [on the Cross] in order to establish solidarity even with those who are furthest from grace, we may, as Hans Urs von Balthasar insisted, reasonably hope that all will find salvation. Again, this has nothing to do

---

[8] Ibid., p. 257.

with our perfectibility; it has to do with God's amazing grace.[9]

Bishop Barron seems to have stumbled into several failures in logic here. Presumably, something is reasonable to believe if we can prove it in some way, or at least show from the evidence that it is probable that our belief is true, or that our hope is justified.[10] *From the fact that we do not know for sure whether any particular person who died is in hell, logically it does not necessarily follow that it is likely that no one is in hell at all.* To be sure, we do not have the gift of reading the hearts of individuals, but as we shall see, we do know quite a lot about the fate of humanity in general from Scripture, Sacred Tradition, and human reason. Drawing upon the evidence from these sources, I will endeavor to show in this chapter that *we can indeed know, beyond a reasonable doubt, that some souls — sadly, many souls — are eternally lost.* We just don't know which ones in particular come to that end. In short, I will argue that it is overwhelmingly probable that at least a substantial minority of the human race has and will irrevocably reject God's love.

Moreover, we cannot logically conclude from the fact that in the liturgy we pray for the souls of all the departed that we are entitled to cling to a "reasonable hope" that all souls will be saved. Surely, we pray for all the departed indiscriminately because (again) we do not know the secret depths of any human soul, and so we do not know which individuals might have irrevocably rejected the love of God, and which

---

[9] Ibid

[10] NB: I am not including in this definition of "reasonable beliefs" what philosophers rightly call "self-evident propositions" or "properly basic beliefs"-- beliefs which cannot be "proven," because they are the foundation of all authentic rational demonstrations.

individuals preserved in their hearts even just a tiny spark of faith and love at the moment of their death — enough for God to fan into flame by the Holy Spirit in the life to come. But that anyone in particular might be saved, as far as we know, does not make it likely that everyone, or even almost everyone will be saved. *And again, from Scripture, Tradition, and reason, as we shall see, we can know beyond a reasonable doubt that everyone will not, in fact, be saved. In fact, many will be eternally lost.*

Finally, *the fact that Jesus on the Cross sought out lost souls into the very depths of their experience of separation from God does not imply that it is likely that all souls, ultimately, will positively respond to Him.* After all, hanging on crosses right beside Jesus were two thieves: one who came to repentance and faith in the end, and one who evidently did not. This Gospel episode formed the basis of the famous saying "Two thieves were crucified alongside our Lord: one was saved — don't despair; one was lost — don't presume."

So it seems that there is considerable confusion on this subject. Perhaps (as I discussed in the first chapter of this book) it all stems from seeing God's merciful love and God's justice as irreconcilable opposites, so that the only way to magnify God's mercy is to minimize His justice as much as possible. The fear that seems to grip so many Catholic theologians and writers today is that if Divine Justice consigns anyone to hell, then He cannot be the God of merciful love that we long to believe in.

Divine Mercy for the Damned?

It's interesting that the great modern Catholic saint of Divine Mercy, St. Maria Faustina Kowalska, had a somewhat different perspective on all this. On the one hand, our Lord spoke to her in private revelations and told her of the priority of His Divine Mercy:

I do not want to punish aching mankind, but I desire to heal it, pressing it to My Merciful Heart. I use punishment when they themselves force Me to do so; My hand is reluctant to take hold of the sword of justice. (*Diary* of St. Faustina, entry 1588)

On the other hand, whenever souls do "force" Him to "take hold of the sword of justice," He wields that sword in a way that fully respects human freedom. Jesus said to her:

[When sinful souls] bring all My graces to naught, I begin to be angry with them, leaving them alone and giving them what they want. (Diary, 1728) ... [Saint Faustina wrote] I received a deeper understanding of Divine Mercy. Only the soul that wants it will be damned. God condemns no one. (*Diary*, 1728, and 1452)

These private revelations given to St. Faustina actually fit quite well with what the *Catechism of the Catholic Church* says about hell in entry 1033, calling it a "state of *definitive self-exclusion* from communion with God." In other words, some souls simply *choose* hell as their preferred, final destination!

As a result, St. Faustina was convinced of the reality of hell, and that some souls do indeed willfully and "definitively exclude" themselves from communion with God (see also *Diary* entries 965 and 1396). Like many other saints, she even had a frightening vision of hell and of the miseries of the lost souls there. She wrote: "I am writing this at the command of God, so that no soul may find an excuse by saying there is no hell, or that nobody has ever been there, and so no one can say what it is like." (*Diary*, 741) In the same passage in her *Diary*, St. Faustina even makes an observation about hell tinged with irony, that also serves as a warning: "But I noticed one thing: that most of the souls there are those who disbelieved that there is a hell."

At one point in this vision, St. Faustina says that in hell she saw a "fire that will penetrate the soul and burn without destroying it — a terrible suffering, since it is a purely spiritual fire, lit by God's anger."

Again, we need to remember that God's anger is not an emotion. It's not sheer vindictiveness either, as if His anger ever could be separated from His love. Rather, His anger is a metaphor for His distributive (in the form of retributive) justice and His total opposition to evil, especially unrepentant evil. Remember that the souls condemned to hell actually *deserve* their punishment on the scales of Divine Justice: They have betrayed infinite love without remorse or regret. What "burns" these souls in a spiritual way, we may surmise, is to be unavoidably confronted with the full truth about their evil deeds and their irrevocable rejection of God's love, and to hear Jesus Christ Himself ratify that truth with the words from His parable, "Depart from Me, accursed ones, into the eternal fire which has been prepared for the devil and his angels" (Mt 25:41). In the end, the truth will win out, and God will not be mocked.

Why do Jesus, the apostles, and St. Faustina tell us about hell? Is it just to frighten us into obeying God? Well, indeed, "the fear of the Lord is the beginning of wisdom" (Prov 9:10), but that's only a beginning. And their main purpose in telling us about all this is actually to magnify God's *mercy*. Like any loving parent who warns his children about the dangers of playing with matches, or running across the street without checking the traffic, God wants to preserve us from harm. He wants to preserve us from ultimate self-destruction. His warnings are warnings of the very real dangers that we face, and they're given out of love for us. In fact, God is so merciful that He has even assumed our human condition as Jesus Christ and died on the Cross to save us from such eternal dangers.

In addition, we should remember that some of the saints teach us that *even hell itself is tempered by, and an expression of, Divine Mercy.* For example, St. Faustina, St. Catherine of Siena, and St. John Eudes all taught that, in effect, God is always as merciful to us as we will allow Him to be. Only our own lack of repentance and lack of trust stands in the way. In fact, His mercy reaches right into the depths of hell itself, even for the lost. God still loves them, even in their everlasting rejection of his love. The tragedy is that the souls of the damned let God love them only in the most minimal way.

First, by allowing souls to reject Him and His love forever, God thereby respects human freedom, the dignity of human free will that He gave to us. He will never take away from us the dignity of being able to choose our own destiny. God will never force people to open their hearts to him and repent. He does not want robots or puppets on a string. The only repentance and love relationship worth having with Him is a freely chosen one. One may ask: "But what about those people who will *not* freely choose it?" The answer: God respects the freedom He gave them, and lets them go their own way. He permits them to walk away from His eternal light, and to dwell in the outer darkness instead.

Second, God knows that for souls who truly despise Him, to have to see Him face to face forever would make them even more miserable than their self-chosen exile from Him in hell. Imagine having to spend eternity in close and intimate union with someone you hate! That is why Bl. John Henry Newman once wrote, "Heaven would be hell to the irreligious." In *Paradise Lost*, the poet John Milton quotes Satan voicing the sentiments of all the damned: "Better to reign in hell than serve in heaven." As C.S. Lewis wrote, "The doors of hell are locked on the inside."[11]

The doctrine of Hell, therefore, though it is disconcerting and sad to us, does not contradict the merciful love of God. It is a manifestation not only of Divine Justice, but also of Divine Mercy.

Is There Really Hell to Pay? Doubts and Debates

The doctrine of Hell has been challenged on numerous grounds over the past three centuries. In order to be clear about how this doctrine manifests both the mercy and the justice of God, we need to look closely at each of these objections.

For example, some theologians question the *fairness* of everlasting punishment for temporal crimes. Is it really just for God to punish souls forever for their evil deeds?

We need to remember, however, that God is infinite perfection, and therefore His love for us is infinite. A grievous betrayal of *that kind of love*, without repentance, is surely a relatively infinite crime, justifying an everlasting sentence. Moreover, many of the worst mortal sins have (or at least can have) everlasting effects on their victims. A murder, for example, takes away the only earthly life a person ever has. Or consider the mortal sin of apostasy: to throw away the gift of faith for oneself can be an act of ingratitude of nearly infinite proportions, and to push others to lose their faith means directly to endanger their life-giving relationship with Jesus Christ, and their eternal salvation. Without subsequent

---

[11] C.S. Lewis, *The Problem of Pain* (New York; Touchstone edition, 1976), p. 114.

contrition and confession, it is not hard to see how such misdeeds — with irrevocable effects on their victims — justify the everlasting punishment of their perpetrators; namely, God's permission of their definitive self-exclusion from His heavenly kingdom.

In addition, we must not confuse the reality of everlasting punishment with a personal experience of everlasting *duration* by the damned. Time, as we know it in our universe, is a process of change. But arguably there's no significant change in Hell. Souls are frozen, as it were, in their chosen state of cold-hearted rebellion and hatred for God. There's no longer any possibility for growth, no longer any possibility of repentance. Where there can be no change, there can be no subjective experience of duration such as we know it on this earth. The damned are not unconscious (Scripture and Tradition certainly do not indicate that), but they are in some ways like everlasting statues in the White Witch's ice-castle in Narnia, by their own stubborn refusal to repent. On earth they gave their hearts to the lifeless idols of wealth, power, fame, sex — or even just the idol of their own self-centeredness — until their slavery to those idols was complete. In short, their hardness of heart was fashioned by the continual misuse of their own free will, until they no longer had any freedom left.

In *Hell and the Mercy of God* (2017), Adrian J. Reimers described the state of the damned like this;

> Those who are raised up to the "second death" will be alive, but living for nothing. The hurt they feel is that loss of any hope, the futility of having nothing to do today that

is worth doing. The fire within consumes the heart and soul in boredom, and frustration, and depression.[12]

Since the state that Reimers describes sounds a lot like the kind of existence lived out by many lost souls already in this life, it is not hard to see how those habits can harden over a lifetime, turning their hearts into hearts of stone.

Some Protestant theologians have speculated that perhaps God simply removes from existence altogether the souls of those irrevocably lost in mortal sin — better for Him to euthanize them, so to speak, than permit them to suffer eternal damnation! This is called the doctrine of "annihilation." But there is hardly any trace of evidence either in Scripture or Sacred Tradition that God does such a thing — probably, because, like euthanizing the terminally ill in this life, it would not be as merciful a thing to do as appears at first glance (see Chapter Five, below, on this issue in society today). The damned are lost in self-love, but they are still "selves" in some sense, still "persons," and God still loves them as much as they permit him to. Besides, as F.J. Sheed once wrote: "[W]e have no reason ... to conclude that condemned souls would want annihilation. To me at least it seems that the love of self-carried to that intensity would involve a clinging to self at all costs."[13]

Some have challenged the doctrine of Hell on the grounds that it allegedly contradicts divine omnipotence: *Can't divine love conquer all resistance in the end?* The metaphor of conquest is not a very apt one, I think, since the one thing that divine love will never do is compel our souls to repent. In the animated

---

[12] Adrian J. Reimers, *Hell and the Mercy of God* (Washington, DC: Catholic University of America Press, 2017), p. 203.
[13] Sheed, *Theology for Beginners*, p. 167.

classic film of the fairy tale Sleeping Beauty, the famous theme song refrain was, "True love conquers all," but in that story it did not conquer the frozen heart of Maleficent[14] — and the same is true of those souls who remain stubbornly unrepentant of mortal sin, without remorse for acts of murder, cruelty, apostasy, rape, incest, adultery, greed, and so on. God really does respect our free will to the bitter end, if we insist on bitterness and hatred in the end. In that sense, we might say, He limits the exercise of His own omnipotence over us, for He does not want to force us to love and trust in Him (coercion would not result in real love and trust anyway, which, to be authentic, must always be freely given. As we said before: robots and puppets on a string cannot love). That self-limitation on God's part is an act of His respect for us and His love for us.

The heart of the believer goes out to the lost in torment in Hell, and that sentiment is certainly an admirable one. Some may ask: "Can Jesus, who proved how passionately He loved us by suffering and dying for us, ignore forever the cries of anguish of those who are lost?" But I think we must be careful not to *romanticize* the cries of the damned. They are not cries of anguish in the sense one might imagine; that is, pleas of poor sufferers who are calling to heaven for relief and compassion. On the contrary, as our Lord says repeatedly, in Hell there is "weeping and gnashing of teeth" — gnashing of teeth: a metaphor for ferocious hatred. Try gnashing your

---

[14] The Disney remake of *Sleeping Beauty* that appeared many decades later, titled *Maleficent*, sought to put a whole new spin on the whole story, claiming that the evil queen as a youth actually had been the innocent victim of betrayal by her lover — and portrayed her heart as redeemable, and redeemed in the end. But this is to make of her a very different character from the one we see in the original, animated version of the story.

teeth in front of a mirror someday, and you'll see what He means! The damned certainly do not weep for their sins, nor do they weep at all for those whom they abused and tormented on earth, and whose earthly lives they shattered. They weep only for themselves. Their cries, as St. Faustina heard in one of her revelations, are cries "of horrible despair, hatred of God, vile words, curses, and blasphemies" (*Diary*, 741). Above all, they blame God for everything. If Jesus were to reach down to the pit of hell to pull them out, they would spit on His hand. Our Lord must surely ignore their curses and their blasphemies, for such cries have no right to be heard.

This whole question strikes close to home, however, for most of us wonder how we ourselves could be happy in heaven knowing that some of the friends and loved ones we cherished on earth are tormented forever in hell. Again, we need to remember that that our Lord's merciful love for these souls is much greater than our own. He knows which souls, in the depths of their hearts, definitively rejected His love and remained stubbornly impenitent and cold-hearted to the bitter end. He knows which souls slammed the door of their hearts and locked them tight. And in His love for them, He will not take away their freedom to do that by kicking those doors down. Moreover, He knows that those lost souls would actually be more miserable in heaven: living in the light of His love which they detest, rather than in their self-chosen exile from him in hell. Besides, as C.S. Lewis once pointed out, what we loved and cherished about them in this life no longer exists: their occasional good humor, their creativity, their affection, and their sparks of authentic love for others — they put these good qualities within them to death, step by step, casualties of their spiritual self-destruction. What carries on in existence in hell, therefore, is a mere shadow of the persons we once knew: mere fragments and "remains," as Lewis put it. If we came face to face with them, we would hardly know them at all, and they would certainly no longer have any love for us.

Some theologians question whether the doctrine of hell really fits with our understanding of divine omniscience: the doctrine that God knows everything that can be known. They reason: *If an all-loving and all-knowing God can foresee that a person will end up in hell forever, why would he bother to create that person?*

The answer to this question is not easy, because it depends upon a proper understanding of God's relationship to time, a difficult philosophical matter.[15]

As St. Thomas Aquinas taught (confirmed by the Church at the First Vatican Council, and alluded to in Catechism 600), God is not bound to "linear time" as we are. He is completely outside of time. So he does not have to "remember" the past nor "look ahead" to "foresee" the future. Rather, all times are present before his eyes at once, so to speak. Saint Thomas described it as like a man looking down from a high citadel on a line of passers-by below. He sees the whole line at once, and which ones are at the head of the line and which ones are toward the back, but again, he also sees the whole line from beginning to end in one simple, constant, gaze.

This means that when God creates the world, and later (in our linear time scale) when he creates you and me, he does not "foresee" or accurately predict whether we will go to heaven or hell, and then need to decide whether or not we are worth creating at all. He knows from all eternity who finally chooses to go to heaven, and who finally chooses to go to hell,

---

[15] For a clear and in-depth discussion of the mystery of God's relationship with time, see Fr. Chris Alar, MIC, *After Suicide: There's Hope for Them and Hope for You* (Stockbridge, MA: Marian Press, 2019), p. 179-195.

because he *actually sees us choosing it*. The future is present to his eyes because it is actual for him, not just possible. Again, he does not "foresee" what you will do tomorrow with your free will — from all eternity, he actually watches you doing it. The same with the past: he does not "remember" what you did yesterday with your free will: from all eternity, he watches you doing it.

Thus the only way that God knows that someone in linear time is going to hell is because he sees them actually choosing to go there, an event in their life always open to his all-encompassing sight. As the ancient Christian philosopher Boethius pointed out, if God could "foresee" (that is, accurately predict) what we would do in the future, then we would not have real free-will, because we would not be free to do otherwise. But God does not "foresee" or "accurately predict": from his eternal vantage point, he just sees how we are using our free will at every moment of our lives. That's how he knows who ultimately chooses heaven and who ultimately chooses hell. The moment of our lives when we freely and finally make that irrevocable choice is always present before him.

So, to understand this matter correctly, the real question is not "Why did God create person X if he 'foresaw' that they were going to be eternally lost?", but "Why did he create creatures like us with free-will at all, knowing full well that some of us would misuse our freedom and end up in a state of irrevocable, spiritual self-destruction? Was it worth it?"

We are not omniscient, so we are in no position to judge. But if it was not worth it, God certainly would not have created us. Jesus frequently alludes to the value and worth of *every human being:* for example "Look at the birds of the air ….are you not of more value than they?" (Mt 6:26, cf. 10:31), and "There will be more joy in heaven over one sinner who repents than over the ninety-nine righteous persons who need no repentance" (Lk 15:7). Also, from what we can surmise, if the solid majority of people use their life on earth freely to receive and cooperate with his grace, and end up in Heaven in the end, enjoying and returning His infinite love forever, that would certainly make humanity worthwhile overall (we will return to this issue later in this chapter). Moreover, even damned souls are not completely worthless: that is why God forever respects the dignity of the free will He gave them and treats them with what compassion He can.

Are we able to peer any more deeply into this mystery? I am not sure that we can, but at least we can trust that God's decision to create humanity, and hold us in existence at every moment, came from the very depths of His wisdom and merciful love.

Then, of course, there is the challenge to the reality of eternal loss on the basis of Holy Scripture. As we have seen, Balthasar and Kasper argue that the biblical witness on this matter is paradoxical, or at least ambiguous. They claim that in some passages Scripture seems to hold out the hope of everlasting salvation for all, while in other places it warns of the danger of everlasting damnation. But nowhere (so they say) does Scripture declare definitively that all will be saved, or that some will be lost. Thus far, the Bible (allegedly) leaves the matter a mystery.

Reason, Scripture and Tradition all Declare the Sobering Truth

I do not relish the task of openly disagreeing again with some of the best writers in the Church today — but it cannot be helped. For it seems to me that *the clear testimony of Scripture, Tradition, and Reason — all three — make it true beyond any reasonable doubt that some souls (indeed, many) are eternally lost, that they irrevocably turn their backs on God's love.*

First, the witness of *Reason*. As we have seen, it is reasonable to believe that all souls are truly free to turn their backs on the light of God, and that God always respects that created freedom He gave us. Everyone on all sides of this debate agrees at least on this point. But if *all* of the roughly 110-billion people who have lived and died on this earth so far definitively chose to embrace His love and light in the end, and *none* ultimately chose to reject Him that would make it pretty hard to believe that they were really free to do otherwise.

Granted that (whether we know it or not) union with God's light and love is our deepest heart's desire, and that His grace is always near at hand to help us (if only we will cooperate with it), nevertheless, throughout this life we still struggle with (a) the inherited wound of original sin, which leaves every one of us burdened with severely disordered passions and desires, from our infancy onward; (b) the constant spiritual assaults and temptations of Satan and the demons; and (c) the corrosive after-effects of our own sins and those of others. For example, most people grow up in a cultural environment that is at least non-Christian, if not downright anti-Christian; the physical and emotional abuse suffered by many, and the false values, bad examples, and peer pressure that our society imposes upon all of us from early childhood immensely influences each one of us to wander from the path of Christ. Given all this, it seems highly unlikely that human freedom, operating in this overall context, is invariably going to choose to embrace the Light. The doctrine of a "legitimate" and "reasonable hope" for universal salvation, therefore, just runs up against the reality of human free will in a fallen world.

Over and against this free will argument, Cardinal Kasper (as we have already seen) set the reflections of St. Edith Stein. In an unpublished manuscript she speculated that the eternal loss of any soul is "in reality … infinitely improbable," since God may be able to "outwit" every soul in the end into choosing to embrace His love. Here are her precise words:

> And now, can we assume that there are souls that remain *perpetually* closed to [divine] love? As a possibility in principle, this cannot be rejected. In reality, it can become *infinitely improbable* — precisely through what preparatory grace is capable of effecting in the soul. … Human freedom can be neither broken nor neutralized by divine freedom, but it may well be, so to speak, *outwitted*.[16]

In other words, the idea seems to be that over time, *in the next life* (as it clearly does not always happen in this present life) God may be able simply to *wear down the resistance* of impenitent souls to the advances of His love — in which case, it would seem that there is no eternal state of hell at all, just a kind of temporary holding-tank for the stubbornly impenitent where God ultimately breaks down their resistance, brings them to repentance and into a state of grace, and then, presumably, ushers them from there into Purgatory or Heaven.

The trouble is that the Church's magisterium has definitively rejected the idea that hell is only a temporary state for some or all of those who go there. Indeed, *Catechism* entries 1033 and 1035 tell us that hell is actually eternal separation from God: "*To die in mortal sin without repenting and accepting God's merciful love* means remaining separated from him *forever* by our own free choice. … *hell is eternal separation from God*, in whom alone man can possess the life and happiness for which he was created and for which he longs" (my emphasis). In other words, St. Edith Stein's speculation about universal salvation would only

---

16 Cited in Ralph Martin, *Will Many Be Saved?* (Grand Rapids: Eerdmans, 2012), p. 139; italics mine

work as a theory in a Catholic context if we could believe that no soul ever dies in mortal sin. For according to authoritative magisterial Tradition, any soul that does die in mortal sin remains in hell forever. Moreover, the eternity of hell is implied in Christ's Parable of the Sheep and the Goats (Mt 25:41, 46). There He expresses the fate of the blessed and the damned on the Judgment Day by using the same Greek word for both destinies: *aionis* (everlasting). In other words, the everlasting reward of the righteous and the everlasting punishment of the wicked are comparable to each other: they are final, everlasting destinies, not temporary states. In addition, St. Paul and the apostles taught us that the time to make a fundamental decision for or against the love of Jesus Christ is right now, in this life, not in some extended time for conversion in the next life:

> Besides this you know what hour it is, how it is full time now for you to wake from sleep. For salvation is nearer to us now than when we first believed; the night is far gone, the day is at hand. Let us then cast off the works of darkness and put on the armor of light .... (Rom 13:11-12; cf. Heb 9:27)

In short, there is no clear indication in the New Testament or Catholic teaching for the idea that there are extended chances for conversion from mortal sin in the next life, or that hell can be merely a temporary state for souls still struggling to attain that basic conversion, or that all souls simply go to Purgatory after death, even those who have fundamentally rejected God's love in this life and died in a state of unrepented mortal sin (on who goes to Purgatory, and why, see the previous chapter of this book).

It follows that to rescue St. Edith Stein's speculations on universal salvation, we would have to squeeze into this present, earthly life the time needed for God's love ultimately to wear down the resistance of all impenitent souls and "outwit" them into repentance and faith. But, again, that would require us to believe that no soul ever really dies in unrepented mortal sin — a belief for which there is not the slightest evidence in Holy Scripture, and a belief that would make a mockery of the Church's traditional teaching on the final judgment (summarized in *Catechism*, entries 1033 and 1035, quoted above).

Besides, St. Edith Stein's reflections on this mystery were merely speculative: the fact that she never had them published may be an indication that she was not sure of their validity. Her speculations might carry some weight if lost souls ended up in hell only because of false-thinking. God could then "outwit" them in the end into changing their minds. But the damned are trapped in their sins not only by their false-thinking, that is, by their self-serving delusions that God does not exist, or that He is neither just nor merciful ("God is not just, so there is nothing to fear" — or "God is not merciful, so there is nothing to hope for"). Rather, even more than their mental errors, they are enslaved by their recalcitrant will, their stubborn, self-inflicted hardness of heart.

The ancient Greek philosophers believed that virtue is attainable solely through acquiring better knowledge. They taught that once you know the truth, you will live accordingly. If that were so, then repentance and conversion would be something we could accomplish by our heads alone. From St. Paul, through St. Augustine and St. John Paul II, however, the Catholic saints have peered deeply into the mystery of iniquity in the human heart. What they discovered is that knowledge of the truth is not enough to save us. The will must be transformed by grace: we must allow our Savior to perform *radical heart surgery* in our innermost depths, if we are to have any chance of reuniting with Divine Love. And this radical inner healing is surely not something that God will force upon anyone. Saint Paul summed up both our predicament and our hope when he wrote to the Romans: "I do not do the good I want, but the evil I do not want is what I do. ... Wretched man that I am! Who will deliver me from this body of death? Thanks be to God through Jesus Christ our Lord!" (Rom 7:19, 24-25).

So we come back to where we started on this point. The free will argument implies that it is overwhelmingly probable — in other words, true beyond a reasonable doubt — that at least some human souls (indeed, many) will freely choose to reject God, and irrevocably harden their hearts to His Love. C.S. Lewis summed it up best in his book, *The Problem of Pain:*

> In the long run, the answer to all those who object to the doctrine of hell is itself a question. What are you asking God to do? To wipe out their past sins and at all costs to give them a fresh start, smoothing over every difficulty and offering every miraculous help? But He has done so, on Calvary. To forgive them? They will not repent and be forgiven. To leave them alone? Alas, I'm afraid, that is what He does."[17]

In addition to the strong probability, based on Reason, that some souls will be lost, we have the witness of *Holy Scripture.* Here we do not need to concede to Balthasar and Kasper that the biblical testimony is paradoxical or ambiguous on this issue. We have our Lord's own warnings in the gospels about the dangers of eternal damnation (some of which we have already quoted in this chapter). In fact, no one in the Bible speaks more often or more emphatically on this subject than Jesus Himself.

---

[17] Lewis, *The Problem of Pain*, p. 114.

Balthasar and Kasper argue that these teachings (which often occur in the form of parables) can be interpreted as mere "cautionary tales"— in other words, they describe what *could* happen to people if they do not repent, without declaring for sure that anyone actually will suffer that fate.

Even if we were to concede that all of our Lord's statements about hell could be explained away in that fashion, however, (and that's a tall order in some cases, such as Mt 16:27, 25: 31-46, 26:24; and Lk 13:27-28) we would still be left with a big problem: Jesus then could be accused of misleading His hearers. If all of His teachings on hell were intended merely as warnings, and not also in some cases as declaratory statements about eternal loss, then why did He never clearly say so? Or even clearly imply it? — not even once! The net result was to mislead all of his apostles and to confuse almost the entire Church about the afterlife for the better part of 2,000 years! Catholic theologian Germain Grisez put it this way:

> In suggesting that Jesus' warnings ... may have been empty threats, von Balthasar implies that Jesus himself may have misrepresented the Father, making him seem other than Jesus knew him to be. But the Holy Spirit cannot have lied, and Jesus cannot have misrepresented the Father. So, von Balthasar's attempt to deal with those Scripture passages is unacceptable.[18]

In other words, if the Father's love really can and will "outwit" and save everyone, Jesus was morally remiss never, not even once, clearly to state or imply it — and numerous times to imply just the opposite.

---

[18] Cited in Martin, *Will Many Be Saved*, p. 145.

By the way, this also applies to Marcus Borg's theory (discussed earlier in this chapter) that Jesus consciously may have adapted the mythical worldview of His ancient audience as a mere pedagogical device: "You folks who believe that some souls will be eternally lost, what do you think the basis of their eternal condemnation would be?" To speak in that way once or twice might be understandable. But to do so over and over again, without even once indicating His true belief that the Father's love will be able to save everyone in the end, was surely grossly irresponsible.

Balthasar pointed to several New Testament passages that seem at first glance to hold out the hope of universal salvation. On closer examination, however, none of them do so very clearly. For example, in John 12:32, Jesus said, "and I, when I am lifted up from the earth, will draw all men to myself." But in the very same chapter, our Lord makes it clear that He did not mean by this that there will be a universal assent to His message, and to His offer of salvation. All will be drawn to him, but some who are drawn will reject him, and become liable to judgment. In verse 48, He says: "He who rejects me and does not receive my sayings has a judge; the word that I have spoken will be his judge on the last day" (the NAB here has "the word that I spoke, it will condemn him on the last day" — and notice: not "may" condemn him or "could" condemn him, but "will"). Given the passage that I also quoted from St. John's Gospel earlier in this chapter about the final resurrection to life and to judgment (5:28-29), it seems pretty clear that according to St. John, Jesus did not hold out any hope for universal salvation.

Some New Testament passages outside of the gospels cannot plausibly be explained away as mere warnings: they are also declarations about the final judgment and ultimate destinies of souls. For example, St. Paul wrote in II Thessalonians 1:7-10 of the coming day when "the Lord Jesus is revealed from heaven with his mighty angels in flaming fire, inflicting vengeance on those who do not know God and upon those who do not obey the gospel of our Lord Jesus. They shall suffer the punishment of eternal destruction and exclusion from the presence of the Lord and the glory of his might ....."[19] Paul wrote here of what *will* happen, not what *may* happen. Saint Jude in verse 7 of his Epistle refers to the eternal punishment of souls from Sodom and Gomorrah, a sentence of damnation that has *already been implemented*, when he says they "serve as an example by undergoing a punishment of eternal fire." No mere warning here about the mere possibility of eternal loss — for these souls are already experiencing it!

In Ephesians 1:10, St. Paul states that God's plan is to "unite all things" in Christ. But this passage has a parallel in Colossians 1:20, where St. Paul wrote that God's plan is "through [Christ] to reconcile to himself all things, whether on earth or in heaven." Notice that he did not include all things "under the earth," which was the traditional, geographical metaphor for Hades or Sheol, a place which, after Christ's descent to liberate the souls of the righteous there and bring them to Heaven, was usually called "hell" by Christians — simply because the only souls left behind there were the lost souls in torment.

---

[19] By "those who do not know God" who will be lost, Saint Paul is referring to those who do not "know" Him by *personal experience*, and who do not respond to that experience of Him by repentance and obedience. He is not saying that all those who do not know explicitly *the gospel message about God and Christ* necessarily will be lost. Those who through no fault of their own never hear or receive the gospel can still be led by divine grace to salvation. See *Catechism* 847, and Acts 14:16; 17:26-28.

In Philippians 2: 10-11, St. Paul foresees that finally "at the name of Jesus every knee would bow, in heaven and on earth and under the earth, and every tongue confess that Jesus Christ is Lord, to the glory of God the Father." In other words, all will one day openly acknowledge the truth about the divine Lordship of Jesus — but this does not necessarily mean that Satan, the demons, and the lost souls in the underworld will make this acknowledgment in a *saving* way (see Jas 2:19). Nowhere does the New Testament hold out any hope for the salvation of those fallen angels and lost souls left in the underworld,[20] where in torment they await the final Judgment Day — and in several places the New Testament implies their eternal punishment (e.g. Mt 25:41, Rev 20:13-14).

We also have several statements in Scripture from apocalyptic prophecy. One of the characteristics of the "apocalyptic" kind of prophecy is that it usually tells us not what *may* happen, conditionally, if people repent or fail to repent, but what God *certainly will do.* It often takes the form of visionary glimpses of the future acts of God. These passages make it clear that some people will remain stubbornly impenitent to the very end of their lives, and as a result will be eternally lost. The prophecy from St. Paul from II Thess 1:7-10 (quoted above) is a good case in point. While filled with symbolism and metaphor, such apocalyptic prophecies are not devoid of doctrinal content, which in some cases is fairly easy to discern:

---

[20] As discussed in the previous chapter, the "underworld" or the expression "under the earth" are metaphors for the spiritual bondage, confinement and darkness of souls in a state of unrepentance and unbelief. It is a purely spiritual dimension of existence, whether in Sheol, before the death and Resurrection of Christ, or in Purgatory or Hell now.

- Daniel 12: 2: "Many of those who sleep in the dust of the earth shall awake, some to shame and everlasting contempt. And those who are wise shall shine ... like the stars forever and ever."
- Revelation 14: 9-12: "If anyone worships the beast and its image, and receives a mark on his forehead or on his hand, he also shall drink the wine of God's wrath, poured unmixed into the cup of His anger, and he shall be tormented with fire and sulfur in the presence of the holy angels and in the presence of the Lamb. And the smoke of their torment goes up forever and ever, and they have no rest day or night, these worshippers of the beast and his image ... ."
- Revelation 20:7-10, 13-15: " And when the thousand years are ended, Satan will be released from his prison, and will come out to deceive the nations .... [A]nd the devil who had deceived them was thrown into the lake of fire and brimstone where the beast and the false prophet were, and they will be tormented day and night for ever and ever. ... Death and Hades gave up the dead in them all, and all were judged by what they had done. Then Death and Hades were thrown into the lake of fire. This is the second death, the lake of fire; and if anyone's name was not found written in the book of life, he was thrown into the lake of fire.

We do not need to take all the symbolism and imagery in these prophecies *literally*, of course. But we do need to take these prophecies *seriously*. The message that the biblical authors were trying to convey here was not that hell literally consists of fire and brimstone, but that after death the wicked will be held accountable before Divine Justice for their evil deeds, and their ultimate fate will be irrevocable, and dreadful beyond imagining.

Finally, we have the testimony of *Sacred Tradition*, the work of the Holy Spirit in the life of the Church. This is found in the liturgies and devotions of the People of God, the witness of the saints and the Fathers, and above all in the teachings of the Ecumenical Councils and Papal Decrees. In a nutshell, the balance of Catholic Tradition tells us that by dying in mortal sin without repentance, some souls will in fact choose "definitive self-exclusion from communion with God" (*Catechism* entry 1453).

The *magisterial* Tradition (that is, those Councils and Papal Decrees) repeatedly implies this. Cardinal Avery Dulles summarized that Tradition for us:

> The constant teaching of the Catholic Church supports the idea that there are two classes: the saved and the damned. Three General Councils of the Church (Lyons I, 1245, Lyons II, 1274, and Florence, 1434) and Pope Benedict XII's bull *Benedictus Deus* (1336) have taught that everyone who dies in mortal sin goes immediately to suffer the eternal punishments of hell. This belief has endured without question in the Catholic Church to this day, and is repeated almost verbatim in *The Catechism of the Catholic Church* (CCC 1022, 1035).[21]

There is no hint anywhere in these magisterial documents that Holy Scripture contradicts itself or is ambiguous about the eternal destiny of human beings, or that we have any reasonable grounds for hope that no one ever dies in a state of unrepented mortal sin, so that all will be saved in the end. Lest there be any doubt on this point, the Vatican's Congregation for the Doctrine of the Faith in 1979 issued a "Letter on Certain Questions Concerning Eschatology," which stated:

> In fidelity to the New Testament and Tradition, the Church believes in the happiness of the just who will one day be with Christ. She believes that there will be [Notice:

"will be" not "may be"] eternal punishment for the sinner, who will be deprived of the sight of God, and that this punishment will have repercussions on the whole being of the sinner.[22]

In addition, some of the saints down through the ages have been granted visions of hell, visions which clearly show that hell is eternally *occupied*, not *empty*. For example, we have the vision received by St. Faustina, quoted earlier in this chapter (from her *Diary*, entry 741). We also have the famous vision of the children of Fatima (recorded in the words of one of the three, Sr. Lucia):

> A few moments after arriving at the Cova da Iria, near the holmoak, where a large number of people were praying the Rosary, we saw the flash of light once more, and a moment later our Lady appeared. ...

> She opened her hands once more, as she had done during the two previous months. The rays of light seemed to penetrate the earth, and we saw, as it were, a sea of fire. Plunged in the fire were demons and souls in human form, like transparent burning embers, all blackened or burnished bronze, floating about in the conflagration, now raised into the air by the flames that issued from within themselves together with great clouds of smoke, now falling back on every side like sparks in a huge fire, without weight or equilibrium, amid shrieks and groans of pain and despair, which horrified us and made us tremble with fear. ...

Terrified and as if to plead for succor, we looked up to Our Lady, who said to us kindly and sadly:

---

[22] Cited in Martin, *Will Many Be Saved?*, p. 182.

You have seen hell where the souls of poor sinners go. To save them, God wishes to establish in the world devotion to my Immaculate Heart. If what I say to you is done, many souls will be saved and there will be peace. ...

When you pray the Rosary, say after each mystery: O my Jesus, forgive us our sins, save us from the fires of hell, and lead all souls to heaven, especially those who are most in need of Thy mercy.[23]

The private revelations given to any particular saint, of course, are not infallible. Indeed, even saints can misinterpret what they believe they have received from God or can color them with their own psychological projections. However, given that "saints" are persons who are full to overflowing with the Holy Spirit, the Spirit of Truth, when you have similar revelations received by numerous saints, from many different times and places, it strains credulity to believe that all this sheer fantasy. There is no category in Catholic theology entitled "the concurrent delusions of the saints"!

In short, in the light of the witness of Reason, Holy Scripture, and Sacred Tradition, it would be rash and imprudent to hold out a "legitimate

---

[23] This statement by our Lady should not be read as implying that to be saved "from the fires of hell" means to be "saved by being taken out of hell." The "us" in this prayer clearly means those saying the prayer itself, and the plea to "lead all souls to heaven" refers to all souls presently living and struggling throughout the world. Neither the children of Fatima nor the Church that examined the facts about this apparition of Mary ever understood her words to have any other meaning. On the other hand, her words at Fatima do imply that we can have the hope that if we all pray with great fervor of faith and love for the living, and offer sacrifices for them, then Jesus will be able to "lead all souls to heaven" who are alive right now.

hope" or "reasonable hope" that all souls will, in the end, be saved. On the contrary, put this three-part witness together, and we can surely know, beyond any reasonable doubt, that at least some souls, and most likely many, will in the end be lost.

Why This Doctrine Makes a Hell of a Difference

Let's recap what we have established so far in this chapter on the divinely revealed truth about hell.

To argue for the sobering reality of everlasting loss is not to undermine or contradict Divine Mercy. Quite the contrary: The Lord is merciful even to the damned, for He eternally respects their freedom to say "no" to Him. In fact, their irreversible decision to "turn their backs" on His light and love, and their resulting just punishment in hell, is actually less miserable to them than having to look into the eyes of Divine Love for all eternity — a love that they cannot stand, and utterly despise. These souls are actually better off in the outer darkness than in the full light of Heaven. Thus, God's mercy extends even to the depths of hell itself, for His mercy and His justice can never be separated in the infinite simplicity of the divine nature (a defined doctrine of the Church). Furthermore, God's merciful love is so great that He even suffered and died for us on the Cross, in the person of His Son, to save us from the misery of rejecting His love forever — if only we will repent and believe.

Many people wonder whether the majority of mankind will end up in heaven or in hell. After all, many great saints have speculated that most souls will be lost in the end and only a small minority will be saved; to name a few: St. Augustine, St. Albert the Great, St. Bernard of Clairvaux, St. Thomas Aquinas, St. Theresa of Avila, and St. Alphonsus Liguori. Saint Leonard of Port Maurice, for example, once preached a homily titled "The Small Number of Those Who are Saved."

This opinion was largely based on our Lord's own words in the gospels:

> Enter through the narrow gate; for the gate is wide and the way is broad that leads to destruction, and there are many who enter through it. For the gate is small and the way is narrow that leads to life, and there are few who find it (Mt 7:13-14).

> And someone said to Him, "Lord, are there just a few who are being saved?" And He said to them, "Strive to enter through the narrow door; for many, I tell you, will seek to enter and will not be able" (Lk 13:23-24).

However, some of these saints and doctors of the Church did not claim to know for sure the proportion of humanity that will be saved, and the Church has never issued a doctrinal definition on the subject. So there is room for alternative opinions here. After all, it does not seem to fit very well with our belief in the infinite power and wisdom of God's merciful love to hold that His plan of salvation was so poorly conceived, or so poorly executed, that the solid majority of humanity will miss out on its eternal benefits!

Moreover, in centuries past theologians may have been reading more into our Lord's words here than He really intended. Jesus said that only a "few" will travel the hard path to eternal life. By that, perhaps He meant that only a few will go straight to heaven when they die, while "many" will follow the path that leads to eternal "destruction" — meaning, perhaps, that many more are following the direct road to hell. But for neither group did He use the word "most," and He did not mention Purgatory here at all. Thus, it does not contradict Christ's teaching to believe that while "few" attain eternal life immediately upon their death, and "many" eternal loss, "most" (perhaps the majority) will actually go to

Purgatory for a time of painful purification and spiritual healing — and then, after that, attain heaven at the last.

In his encyclical "Saved in Hope" (*Spe Salvi*), Pope Benedict XVI encouraged this perspective. Bishop Robert Barron has written in the past in defense of Pope Benedict's teaching on this point.[24] For instance, in an article entitled "Saving the Hell out of You" posted on his website wordonfire.org, Barron stated:

> Sections 45-47 of the Pope's 2007 encyclical ... can be summarized as follows. There is a relative handful of truly wicked people in whom the love of God and neighbor has been totally extinguished through sin, and there is a relative handful of people whose lives are utterly pure, completely given over to the demands of love.
>
> Those latter few will proceed, upon death, directly to Heaven, while those former few, will, upon death, enter the state the Church calls Hell. But the Pope concludes that "the great majority of people," who, though sinners, still retain a fundamental ordering to God, can and will be brought to Heaven after the necessary purification of Purgatory. ...
>
> It seems to me that Pope Benedict's position — affirming the reality of Hell but seriously questioning whether the vast majority of human beings ends up there — is the most tenable and actually the most evangelically promising.

Well, I am *almost* in full agreement with the speculations offered by Pope Benedict and Bishop Barron here (I call them

---

[24] I say "in the past," because this article no longer seems to be available on his "Word on Fire" website.

"speculations," because the Holy Father clearly did not intend to make a definitive doctrinal statement on this subject in his encyclical; he prefaced his remarks on the matter with the words, "We may suppose ... "). I am not quite in full agreement with this view, because our Lord did (not) say that only a "few" or only a "handful" will be eternally lost, but "many." That surely implies at least a substantial minority of the human race. It was certainly way too many for His merciful Heart to bear without shedding blood, sweat, and tears in the Garden of Gethsemane, a crushing sorrow caused in part by His foresight of the multitudes who would be lost, despite His loving Passion and Death for them.[25]

This debate is no mere academic exercise. For unless "many" are in a real and present danger of eternal loss, the Church's historic task of evangelism does not make much sense. In a recent and influential book on the subject, titled *Will Many Be Saved?*, Dr. Ralph Martin argues that if salvation is guaranteed to virtually everyone, Catholics are not likely to be filled with a passion to spread the gospel around the world with any urgency — much less to make the kind of personal sacrifices often needed to bring unbelievers to Christ. (Think, for example, of the horrible sufferings endured in the 17th century by the Jesuit Martyrs of North America). If the New Evangelization is really to get off the ground, and proceed with real energy and urgency, it needs to be propelled by teaching about heaven and hell that recognizes the real

---

[25] That in the Garden Jesus suffered intense grief from his vision of the eternal loss of so many souls is a truth corroborated by the reflections and private revelations of many saints and holy souls of the Church, including Bl. Anne Catherine Emmerich, St. John Eudes, St. Margaret Mary Alacoque, St. Alphonsus De Liguori, and St. Padre Pio.

dangers we face from our stubborn lack of repentance and faith.

The bishops at Vatican II shared this same concern. In the council document *Lumen Gentium*, section 16, they stated that there are some people in a state of "invincible ignorance" of the truth of the Catholic faith who ultimately can be saved by divine grace, if they respond positively to those rays of the light of truth to which they have access — but, the Council fathers warned that "very often" this does not happen. All too often, those without the light of the Catholic faith are "deceived by the Evil One," live and die "without God" and are exposed to "ultimate despair."[26] This is one reason given why the gospel of "salvation" must be preached to all the world, they said. In other words, according to Vatican II, eternal loss is a clear and present danger to multitudes of people alive today, and one reason for the urgency of the Church's mission.

At the same time, Vatican II did not put the doctrine of hell "front and center" as the best way to communicate the gospel to the world in our time. Much like the Gospel according to St. Luke, Vatican II reminded Catholics of the sobering reality of everlasting damnation, while placing the emphasis of the gospel message elsewhere: namely, on the *positive fruits* of faith in Jesus Christ *in this present life* — forgiveness and grace, healing and sanctification, social justice and peace — *and in the life to come: eternal life with God in heaven.* In other words, the gospel message should focus on what the Church calls "integral salvation": the dawning of the Kingdom of God on earth and its completion in heaven.

---

[26] See Appendix B for further discussion of the prospects for the salvation of non-Catholics.

We find the same focus in the other biblical book written by St. Luke: the Acts of the Apostles. Luke tells us that after St. Peter's first evangelistic homily, 3,000 people were added in one day to the number of those being "saved." Saved from what? Saint Peter tells us in acts 2:40, urging his listeners to save themselves "from this corrupt generation." So in part, salvation is a rescue operation from the emptiness and decadence of the prevailing culture. But in Acts 10:42-43, he speaks also of the salvation that Christ brings in terms of the forgiveness of sins, and as a preparation for the final judgment. In short, the apostles in Acts speak of the good news of integral salvation through Jesus Christ: that the coming of His Kingdom is already beginning on earth through the outpouring of His Holy Spirit in the hearts of those who believe, and in the life of the Church, but that it only comes to full fruition at the end of time, in the heavenly Kingdom. As a result, we are saved by Christ from the "living hell" we might otherwise make for ourselves, both in this life and in the next.

The Social Repercussions of the Doctrines of Divine Justice and Final Judgment

Some theologians worry that if people really believe in Divine Justice and final judgment, this can lead them to commit acts of vengeance and social violence. As Protestant pastor Timothy Keller puts it in his book *The Reason for God*, "If you believe in a God who smites evildoers, you may think it perfectly justified to do some smiting [of evildoers] yourself." But the New Testament clearly teaches that the job of meting out penal justice in its fullness rightly can be done only by God. He alone knows the secrets of all hearts. He alone knows who is truly guilty of what: "'Vengeance is mine, I will repay,' says the Lord" (Rom 12:19). Besides, as Keller reminds us, it was the noted Croatian theologian Miroslav Volf, a man who had personally witnessed the horrible violence of ethnic cleansing in the Balkans, who argued that more often it is *lack of belief in a God of judgment* that "secretly nourishes violence." Keller explains:

> The human impulse to make perpetrators of violence pay for their crimes is almost an overwhelming one. It cannot possibly be overcome with platitudes like "Now don't you see that violence will not solve anything?" If you have seen your home burned down and your relatives killed and raped, such talk is laughable — and it shows no real concern for justice. ...

> Can our passion for justice be honored in a way that does not nurture our desire for blood vengeance? ... The best resource for this is belief in the concept of God's divine justice. If I don't believe that there is a God who will eventually put all things right, I will take up the sword [and try to do it myself] and will be sucked into the endless vortex of retaliation. Only if I am sure that there is a God who will right all wrongs and settle all accounts perfectly do I have the power to refrain.[27]

In addition, Keller quotes Czeslaw Milosz, the Nobel Prize winning poet from Poland, who had this retort to Karl Marx's famous statement that religion is merely "the opiate of the masses":

> A true opium of the people is a belief in nothingness after death — the huge solace of thinking that our betrayals, greed, cowardice, and murders are not going to be judged.

In other words, the true opiate of the masses is the comforting delusion that the wicked cling to — *the delusion that*

---

[27] Timothy Keller, *The Reason for God* (New York: Penguin, 2009), p. 77.

in the end, no one is really answerable to anyone for anything. Keller writes:

> Many people complain that belief in a God of judgment will lead to a more brutal society. Milosz had personally seen, in both Nazism and Communism, that a loss of belief in a God of judgment can lead to brutality. If we are free to shape life and morals any way we choose without ultimate accountability, it can lead to violence. Both Volf and Milosz argue that the doctrine of God's final judgment is a necessary undergirding for human ... peacemaking.[28]

Sadly, as we have seen even mainstream Catholic writers and theologians today tend to press the "mute" button when it comes to the revealed truths of final judgment and the retributive justice of God. This truncates and distorts our understanding the doctrines of Christ's saving work on the Cross and the eternal loss from which He has rescued us. And now we can see that it even has destructive social consequences. Paradoxically, by trying to magnify God's mercy at the expense of His justice, we only end up watering down our appreciation of the depth and power of His merciful love itself.

So, is there a hell? You bet there is. It is the hell that some people fashion for themselves when they turn their backs on the light of the merciful love of God to the very end of their lives, and choose to dwell in the darkness instead. Nevertheless, God mercifully respects the freedom He gave them to the bitter end — even if they choose bitterness and the rejection of His love in the end — and He tempers their misery by not forcing them to gaze on the light of His

---

[28] Ibid., p. 78.

countenance forever. Thus, even the justice of hell is tempered with Divine Mercy.

In fact, our Lord gave His very life for each and every one of us on the Cross, shedding His own blood to obtain our divine pardon, and all the graces we need to rescue us from eternal loss. And He seeks us out as a Good Shepherd who seeks for his lost sheep, even to the very last second of our lives, to save us from irrevocable, spiritual self-destruction. Saint Faustina writes:

> God's mercy sometimes touches the sinner at the last moment in a wondrous and mysterious way. Outwardly, it seems as if everything were lost, but it is not so. The soul, illumined by a ray of God's powerful final grace, turns to God in the last moment with such a power of love that, in an instant, it receives from God forgiveness of sin and punishment, while outwardly it shows no sign either of repentance or contrition, because souls [at that stage] no longer react to external things. Oh, how beyond comprehension is God's mercy! (*Diary*, entry 1698)

But then St. Faustina goes on to relate how for some souls, even this final outpouring of divine grace is not enough:

> But — horror! — there are also souls who voluntarily and consciously reject and scorn this grace! Although a person is at the point of death, the merciful God gives the soul that interior vivid moment, so that if the soul is willing, it has the possibility of returning to God. But sometimes the obduracy in souls is so great that consciously they choose hell; they [thus] make useless all the prayers that other souls offer to God for them and even the efforts of God Himself. (1698)

One thing alone is necessary; that the sinner set ajar the door of his heart, be it ever so little, to let in a ray of God's merciful grace, and then God will do the rest. (1507)

What more could the merciful Jesus possibly do to save us?

Chapter Five
Catholic Social Teaching:
Where Mercy and Social Justice Meet

"Divine Mercy" on the one hand, and "social justice" on the other, are two phrases that rarely seem to be coupled together, and they are even more rarely propagated by the same people. I have often been dismayed by a false dichotomy that one finds all too often in the Church: the division between those on one side who are convinced that cultivating spirituality and piety (including the Divine Mercy message and devotion that comes to us through St. Faustina) is the most important manifestation of God's will for us today, and, on the other hand, those who claim that the struggle for justice and peace in the world is really the most important thing.

But both sides are wrong. The two are inseparable.

In St. Luke's gospel, chapter 11, verse 42, for example, Jesus says: "Woe to you, Pharisees! For you tithe mint and rue and every herb, and neglect justice and the love of God." So Jesus connects the "true" love of God with the seeking of "justice." Both are clearly important to Him, and each one (when it is true and healthy anyway), involves the other. Authentic love for God our Father should lead us to care for the well-being of all His children, and authentic love for our neighbors, our brothers and sisters, needs to be rooted in God's revealed truth, and guided by His Spirit, if it is not to go astray, and do more harm than good.

Let's start with the phrase "social justice." As we saw in the introductory chapter of this book, the biblical concept of "justice" has to do with much more than just courtrooms and lawsuits; rather, "justice" is the right ordering of all things under God, according to God's will — and obviously, that means it is not solely comprised by the right practice of religious piety. Rather, in St. Matthew's report of this saying (Mt 23:23), our Lord includes the practice of "justice, mercy and faith" together, all three, as among "the weightier matters of the law." So religious practices that nurture faith are in that "heavyweight" category for sure, but so also is the practice of justice and mercy.

Over the last century, the Catholic Church has repeatedly called her members not to hide their heads in the sand when it comes to the social and economic injustices that are rife in the crumbling civilization in which we live. We must not retreat into a pious "bunker mentality" — turning ourselves into mere "bunker Catholics" who are so convinced that the world is irreversibly going to hell that all we focus on every day is going to Mass, saying our rosaries, and looking after our own families.

After all, our families are part of a wider socio-economic order (and disorder) that impinges upon our lives every day, and that needs our contribution to the common good if it is not going to take all of us "down with the ship," so to speak: the sinking ship of western civilization all around us.

And that is what Catholic Social Teaching is really all about: it's about legitimate concern for the common good, that is, for some of those "weightier matters of the law" — at least those concerning "social justice" and "peace." It's about Christ's command to love our neighbors as ourselves — when we begin to realize that we actually have many neighbors, not just the people next door. It's about the Lordship of Jesus Christ, who is not only our personal Lord and Savior, but the Lord who wants to reign over every aspect of our lives — including the economic and even political dimensions of our lives.

It follows that Catholic Social Teaching is also about confronting the social idolatries of each and every age. The temptation always exists to turn some aspect of society, or some social ideology into an "idol," that is, to make it our highest authority and first loyalty, over and above our loyalty to Jesus Christ, the rightful Lord of all. Satan always tempts us to give our highest allegiance to some lesser, created reality: to our race and nation (as the Nazis did), to our social class (as the Communists did), to the accumulation of wealth (as the Capitalist robber-barons did), to the social supremacy of our religious institutions (as the Spanish Inquisitors did long ago, and the Ayatollahs in Iran do today), or even to our own absolute autonomy and personal freedom (as the abortionists and Pro-Choice advocates do now). Every act of social idolatry ends up abusing and denigrating others — people who belong to God our Father as His children, made in His image, and who are loved by Jesus Christ, our Savior, who gave His life for us all. The Ven. Archbishop Fulton J. Sheen once warned: "If men do not adore the true Absolute, they will adore a false one"[1] — and the consequences of doing that are always socially destructive.

Of course, the Church never claims to be able to lay out for us a detailed set of economic and social policies, much less a political platform: she teaches general social principles for us to apply to the often complex social realities of our time. Nevertheless, as we shall see, *those social principles are so powerful, and so penetrating, that they offer a genuine, prophetic critique of the world today*, and in some cases, at least, their contemporary application is not really very hard to discern. Moreover, although not a recipe for utopia, if they were followed and implemented, there is little doubt that the world would be a vastly better place than it is now.

---

[1] Cited in Fulton J. Sheen, *Justice and Charity* (Charlotte, NC: ACS Books, 2016), p. 2.

Robert Stackpole

On The Dignity of Every Human Life

The *Compendium of the Social Doctrine of the Catholic Church* (2005), in sections 105-117, tells us that the first and most fundamental social principle is the God-given dignity and worth of every human person. In other words, there are no "throw-away" human beings. People are not reducible to "things," mere objects, "useful" or "useless" to society, to the economy, to the government, or even to ourselves. Rather, we are all "persons," not "things;" from a Christian perspective we are all children of God, in that each one of us is a unique creation of our heavenly Father. Fashioned by Him in His "image" as "persons," — that is, as creatures with the inherent capacity for self-consciousness, rational thought and the exercise of free will — we are capable of using our freedom, with the help of His grace, to grow in His "likeness" in love and wisdom more and more throughout this earthly life, in preparation for the life to come.

This is why God created us. This is His deepest desire, springing from His merciful love for us, a love that always generously seeks to meet our true needs and help us overcome all the miseries that afflict us.

This is also the foundation of our inherent dignity and worth: out of merciful love God made us; out of merciful love He took flesh and dwelt among us in the person of His Son, Jesus Christ; out of merciful love the Son of God preached, healed and suffered, and even died for us on the Cross, that He might merit for us the gift of the Holy Spirit and His sanctifying grace, and pour it into our hearts more and more, until we are fully grown in His likeness, and fully prepared by grace for eternal life with Him in Heaven.

In short, every one of us is made in His image, bought with the price of His own blood, and offered eternal life with Him in Heaven — in other words: we are creatures of inestimable value, because from the first moment of our lives, we are created in His image to be the objects of His merciful love; we are that precious to the Creator and Redeemer of all.

The dignity and worth of every human being is also a central teaching of the Gospel according to St. Luke, "the Gospel of Mercy." Although he certainly did not spell out the full social implications of this principle, Luke clearly believed that the created dignity of every human being was at the heart of the gospel of the Kingdom of God that Jesus Christ both preached and lived. New Testament commentator Rick Torretto pointed out that if we look at the material in Luke, we can see that he deliberately included many stories about Jesus that stress this theme (and some that are unique to St. Luke's gospel).[2] For example, we find:

1. The cure of the servant of a "centurion," who was a military officer from the dreaded Roman army occupying Palestine. So, both slaves and foreign army officers are objects of the love of our Lord.

2. A son is raised to life because he was the only son of a widow of Nain, who would be left destitute without him. Here the love of our Lord goes out to those who are grieving, and those who are falling through the cracks of the social system (since without a husband or a son, this woman would have had no one to provide for her in her old age). This story is found only in St. Luke's gospel.

---

[2] Rick Torretto, "Saint Luke: The Gospel of Divine Mercy" in Robert Stackpole, ed., *Divine Mercy: The Heart of the Gospel* (Stockbridge, MA: Marian Press, 1999), p. 25-26. I am paraphrasing Torretto's list here.

3. A woman of questionable reputation anoints Jesus for burial (so, those who repent of a life of sexual sin are received by our Lord with love and mercy).

4. Female disciples travel with Jesus and support him in his ministry; in this society women were considered second-class citizens who were not usually permitted to travel around with itinerant prophets or rabbis.

5. Jesus tells the Parable of the Good Samaritan, in which a good deed is done by the character in the story from which his Jewish audience would have least expected one: a Samaritan — the Jews considered Samaritans heretical, sectarian half-breeds. This parable is found only in Luke.

6. In the Parable of the Rich Man and Lazarus, a homeless, poor and sick person — among "the lowest of the low" — is welcomed into Abraham's bosom in Heaven. This parable too is found only in Luke.

7. Jesus touches and cures lepers, who really were "the lowest of the low" at that time: they were medical, social, and religious outcasts.

8. In the Parable of the Pharisee and the Tax Collector, the tax collector was praised for his genuine repentance and humility — so even those hated, profiteering collaborators with the Roman occupation could repent and be saved. In the same way, Jesus seeks out and obtains the conversion of the tax collector Zacchaeus. These stories are also unique to St. Luke's gospel.

9. Even those guilty of the worst crime of all — the crime of deicide — are forgiven by Jesus from the Cross: "Father, forgive them, for they know not what they do."

As there are no "throw-away" people at all in St. Luke's

Gospel, so there are no throw-away kinds or classes of people. Religious minorities (such as Samaritans), foreigners (such as the Syro-Phoenician woman and her demon possessed daughter) and immigrants too — recall that the Holy Family were political refugees and immigrants in the land of Egypt — all are precious in God's sight. Even the rich are not to be demonized and treated as sub-human.

Saint Luke's gospel certainly contains a number of teachings of Jesus that tell us about the dangers of wealth. Our Lord warns us that accumulating and hanging on to wealth can hold us in bondage: "No one can serve two masters .... You cannot serve God and wealth" (Lk 16:13 NRSV). Wealth just too easily becomes an idol that claims our highest loyalty, in place of God. So, "Be on your guard against all kinds of greed," Jesus says, "for one's life does not consist in the abundance of possessions" (Lk 12:15 NRSV). Besides, wealth has no eternal value: "You fool," Jesus says in His parable; "This very night your life is demanded of you. And the things you have prepared, whose will they be? So it is with those who store up treasures for themselves, but are not rich toward God" (Luke 12: 16-21 NRSV). The Parable of the Rich Man and Lazarus in Luke chapter 16, of course, is a vivid indictment of those among the wealthy who are cruel and heartless to the poor living right in their own neighborhood, even lying right at their front gate. But our Lord is not preaching class war here, nor even the condemnation of the rich as a whole as a social group. Right after teaching hyperbolically in Luke 18:25 that "it is easier for a camel to go through the eye of a needle than for a rich man to enter the Kingdom of God," Jesus adds this caveat: "What is impossible with men is possible with God." And we see that seeming impossibility become a reality in the conversion story of Zacchaeus in Luke 19, who was certainly a wealthy man, and in the devotion and discipleship of Joseph of Arimathea in Luke 23, who was wealthy and powerful enough to have a seat on the Temple council, and to own a burial cave just outside of the gates of Jerusalem. We see this also even in our Lord's scathing parable about the Rich Man and Lazarus, because Lazarus' compensation for all that he suffered from his poverty was to be welcomed into the bosom of Abraham in Heaven — and Abraham, with all his flocks and herds, was by ancient standards quite a wealthy man.

For Jesus, what matters most is not whether one is rich or poor, but what one actually does with what one has. Fulton Sheen once summed up the true Christian attitude toward wealth in the form of a prophetic exhortation:

All ye who have, remember! [Christ] is walking to your doors on the feet of the hungry; He is asking you for a drink, through the parched tongues of the sick; He is bumping into you at your street corners in the person of a beggar; He is looking in through your windows as a Lazarus as you dine with Dives; His mother is knocking at your portals as Mary did at Bethlehem, asking just for an inn where the Savior might be born. If Bethlehem only knew! If only we suspected! The next time you refuse the poor, ask yourself this question: "What if that man be Christ?"[3]

Of course, St. Luke was not writing a treatise on fundamental human dignity and human rights. But by including in his gospel account so many stories about Christ's love for the poor and the outcast, he surely meant to tell us that there is an inherent, God-given dignity and worth to every person, and indeed every kind of person, even the most socially objectionable and religiously marginalized people. That's why the merciful love of God was offered by Jesus to all, and the only thing that could stop them from accepting this gift of Divine Love was their own refusal to repent and believe.

[3] Sheen, *Justice and Charity*, p. 90.

According to Catholic Social Teaching, *a truly just society is one that respects, protects, and nurtures this God-given worth and dignity of every human being.* Of course, individuals who grossly violate the human dignity of others (e.g., criminals) are to be restrained with the minimum force necessary for the protection of the innocent. Meanwhile, the gift of life is to be guarded and sustained as the foundational gift from God, the one on which our human worth and dignity ultimately is based, and therefore the protection of innocent life is the fundamental "human right;" it is the first responsibility of every society, every social institution, and every government, to uphold and defend that right.

This Church teaching should not sound strange to the ears of Americans. Our Declaration of Independence (in 1776) established that all human beings are "endowed by their Creator" with certain "unalienable rights" (in other words, rights that should never be violated because they come to us from God, not from society), and that chief among these are the rights to "life, liberty, and the pursuit of happiness" — in that order. First of all, without a secure right to "life," all other human rights are in jeopardy (after all, dead people cannot live in "liberty" or "pursue happiness"). Liberty, too, is a fundamental human right, for it enables each of us to use the free will that God gave us, but not at the expense of the lives of others, or the legitimate exercise of liberty by others. "Happiness" — well, not many of the Founding Fathers were Catholics, so what they meant by "happiness" here was all a bit "fuzzy," but it certainly ought to mean not just physical pleasure or economic security and comfort, but human wellbeing in every respect. In that sense, everyone has the social right to use their life and liberty to pursue it, but not in such a way that deprives others of their life, or of the legitimate exercise of their liberty, and their pursuit of happiness.

This hierarchy of fundamental human rights is precisely what made the institution of slavery in America so deplorable. It was a blatant contradiction both of the Catholic Faith and of the founding principles of the United States. Slavery in the United States involved the attempt by some people to "pursue their happiness" by depriving others of their legitimate human "liberty." This clearly violated the dignity of human persons. As far back as 1537, Pope Paul III condemned enforced slavery in his papal bull *Sublimus Deus*, declaring it a moral crime worthy of excommunication, and the Roman Pontiffs never ceased to repeat and extend that teaching in the centuries that followed.[4]

In our own time, the Church has repeatedly spoken out against threats to the dignity of the human person, including the following:

1. *Poverty and Deprivation*. The "right to life" of destitute people is continually threatened by hunger and disease, and clearly such persons cannot exercise much "liberty" in the pursuit of their "happiness" and well-being if they cannot first find adequate food, clothing, shelter, medical care, and employment opportunities. For example, there are some countries that impoverish their own people simply because their economic and political system is chronically unproductive. This is the sad legacy of communist and socialist economies, where wealth creation is stifled by bureaucracy, and political oppression. There are other countries that have economic and political systems that produce plenty of wealth, but it is so unjustly distributed that the "pursuit of happiness" by many, and even the very lives of the poorest members of society, are severely compromised.

---

[4] This papal bull is sometimes cited online as *Sublimus Dei*.

2. *Tyranny and Totalitarianism.* When sovereign states abuse their power and authority, they often treat human beings as mere "pawns" on a political and economic chessboard, rather than as "persons": people end up being treated as mere statistics, mere "things" to be used or abused as their rulers see fit in order to preserve and extend their own power and privileges. Many nations throughout the world still suffer under tyrannical regimes, such as China, Russia, North Korea, Cuba, Venezuela, Iran, and Saudi Arabia, just to name a few.

3. *Terrorism.* The terrorist also treats innocent human beings as mere "things," with no inherent dignity or human rights; innocent members of the general public are continually threatened, and often murdered in order to promote the particular political or religious agenda of the terrorists. Sadly, terrorism has become the "weapon of choice" of radical Islam in our time.

As Catholics, we are certainly called by the Holy Spirit to use our voice and our votes to help keep these social ills from rising and spreading in our world. Threats such as these to the dignity of human life are obvious and widely condemned in the western world, even if much more progress needs to be made in combatting them.

A more subtle, and in that sense more insidious threat to human dignity, however, is now pervasive both in Europe and in North America: the stripping away of the fundamental right to life of those at the very beginning and very end of the human journey, namely unborn children and the terminally ill, through the legalization and social acceptance of abortion and euthanasia. Pope St. John Paul II warned us about this in his great encyclical *Evangelium Vitae* (The Gospel of Life, 1995). Our Lord and Savior Jesus Christ, out of His infinite love and compassion for every human being, is still calling out to us today, through His Body the Church, to become faithful and fervent defenders of the gift of life. This "right to life," according to the Church, extends from conception to its natural end. As Jesus said, it extends especially "to the least of my brethren" (Mt 25:40), whether these helpless and vulnerable ones are unborn children in the womb of their mother, or the terminally ill nearing their journey's end.

A Case in Point: Why "Mercy Killing" is Not Merciful

Take, for example, the issue of euthanasia and physician assisted suicide. In some countries in the world, and in some states in the USA, it is now legal to stop providing food and water to a patient who is terminally ill, or in a seemingly irreversible comatose or vegetative state. This is a serious moral evil that the Church has repeatedly condemned. It is one thing to cease painful or expensive medical treatment that has little chance of significantly improving a patient's condition. The Church has always recognized there is a point at which such medical intervention becomes pointless and burdensome, and that in such cases a person can and should be permitted to die a dignified death, with the assistance of appropriate pain-reducing medications, and the prayers and loving support of family members, friends, and church communities: in other words, with the assistance of proper "palliative care." Food and water, however, do not constitute medical "treatment." They are part of basic human "care" that all of us need at every stage of our life. A person's life journey certainly has not reached its natural end (their natural time to die, in God's providence), if that person can still survive with the basic care of adequate food and water. *Catholics must be aware of this distinction between the "medical treatment" and "basic care" of those terminally ill, and how important it is that we not seek to hasten the process of dying through a deliberate failure to provide that care.* Let's remember that failure to provide this basic care means leaving terminally ill persons literally to die of thirst and starvation — not just from their terminal illness.

Even more alarming is the spread of support for physician-assisted suicide: the right of a physician actively to take a patient's life when that person judges (or, if that person is mentally incapacitated, when his or her relatives' judge) that their life is "no longer worth living." Jesus teaches us through His Church that *there is a profound moral distinction between killing an innocent human being in such a situation (sometimes wrongly termed "mercy killing")* and letting someone die with a degree of comfort and dignity when that person's natural life is clearly drawing to a close.

In other words, *mercy killing is not merciful!* It is the deliberate taking of an innocent human life, and a violation of the dignity and inalienable rights of those who are gravely ill. Even if it is done with the patient's own consent, it is still an attack on innocent human life. Just because something "belongs" to you does not mean you have the moral right to destroy it. For example, a man may be a private art collector and own Renoirs and Picassos. Does that mean he has the moral right to destroy them when he no longer feels they bring him happiness? Of course not. Those works of art are of special value to humanity, no matter what the art collector may now think of them.

In a similar way, the earthly life of each one of us is precious to the God whose "artwork" we are, and who attempts to put the last "brushstrokes," so to speak, on the human soul, working in the very depths of the hearts of each of us when we are nearing the end of our earthly life. The One who entrusted that earthly life to us to begin with, namely our merciful Father and Creator, surely has a plan for the life of each one of us, and surely knows when it is best for us to leave it.

Jesus taught us to "be merciful as your Father is merciful" (Lk 6:36). To be merciful in such a situation is not to take the power of life and death completely away from Him and into our own hands, nor to presume to judge when a person's life is no longer worth living. Who are we to say what kind of struggle for salvation and surrender to the Holy Spirit is going on in the depths of a human soul when they are in a comatose or persistent vegetative state? Who are we to decide to short-circuit that process? Moreover, we must try not give in to the feelings of depression that sometimes overwhelm us when we ourselves are terminally ill—again, we are persons of full value as children of God, made in His image, even if we are no longer actively useful to others (even as passive sufferers, however, we are giving something valuable to others: the opportunity to practice and grow in the virtues of mercy and compassion). Nor are we to give in to feelings of grief and sorrow when we see our loved ones afflicted by terminal illness. Feelings are not always a fully accurate gauge of the truth. The truth is that even the terminally ill are children of God, infinitely loved by Jesus our Savior who "bought" them with "the price of His own blood" (1 Cor 6:20, 7:23), and they are worthy of every legitimate form of palliative care, prayer, and encouragement that we can provide for them. That is the true call of mercy at the end of life's journey.

I wanted to highlight the issues of euthanasia and physician assisted suicide here because I believe these are the next major building blocks of the anti-life culture — the Culture of Death, as St. John Paul II called it — which is gradually coming our way in the United States, and also because these issues are a good illustration of the principle of the Dignity of Every Human Life at the heart of Catholic Social Teaching, especially the lives of the most innocent and helpless human beings.

Solidarity and the Preferential Option for the Poor

A second, essential principle of Catholic Social Teaching is the principle of "Solidarity": this involves *a complete commitment of oneself to the common good.*[5] Pope St. John Paul II elaborated on this principle in his encyclical *Sollicitudo rei Socialis* (On Social Concern, 1987):

> [Solidarity] is not a feeling of vague compassion or shallow distress at the misfortunes of so many people, both near and far. On the contrary, it is a firm and persevering determination to commit oneself to the common good: that is to say, to the good of all and of each individual, because we are all really responsible for all." (section 38)

To put it another way, the answer to Cain's question after he killed his brother Abel, "Am I my brother's keeper?" is simply "Yes, to some extent you really are your brother's, and your neighbor's keeper, at least in the sense of upholding the life and liberty of others, and helping insure that they have access to the basic goods needed for human survival and the pursuit of happiness: such as adequate food, clothing, shelter, medical care, educational and employment opportunities — and, of course, free access to the truth of the gospel (for without the truth of the love of Christ for us, and the help of His grace poured into our hearts through the sacraments, we will never attain that integral happiness and salvation which everyone longs to find).[6]

---

[5] See *Compendium of the Social Doctrine of the Catholic Church* (2005), entry 193.

[6] See the brief discussion of "integral salvation" in Chapter Four of this book.

One of the key expressions of Solidarity is the Catholic social principle sometimes called "the preferential option for the poor," or "the preferential love for the poor," in other words, a preferential concern for their plight: not because they are better than other people, but simply because they often suffer the most, and are most in need. *Catechism* entry 2448 explains it this way;

> In its various forms — material deprivation, unjust oppression, physical and psychological illness and death — human misery ... elicited the compassion of Christ the Savior, who willingly took it upon himself and identified himself with the least of his brethren. Hence, those who are oppressed by poverty are the object of a preferential love on the part of the Church which, since her origin, and in spite of the failings of many of her members, has not ceased to work for their relief, defense, and liberation through numerous works of charity which remain indispensable always and everywhere.

To begin with, this preferential concern for the poor is rooted in our Savior's own earthly ministry. Anyone who has read the gospels in the New Testament will be well aware that Jesus of Nazareth had a special concern for the plight of the poor and the sick, and especially for the most innocent and helpless human beings. It is the foundation of His teaching: "Truly, I say to you, as you did it to one of the least of these my brethren, you did it to me" (Mt 25:40). It is one reason why He healed the leper by the roadside, and the man born blind, and raised up from death the daughter of Jairus, and the son of the widow of Nain.

Above all, Jesus pointed to His miracles of compassion for the suffering and the helpless as the sign that the Kingdom of God was dawning in the world through His own life and work. Saint Luke's gospel in particular highlights this theme

— right from the beginning of our Savior's public ministry (Luke 4: 16-21):

> And He came to Nazareth, where He had been brought up; and He went to the synagogue, as was His custom, on the Sabbath day. And He stood up to read; and there was given to Him the book of the prophet Isaiah. He opened the book and found the place where it was written: "The Spirit of the Lord is upon me, because he has anointed me to preach good news to the poor. He has sent me to proclaim release to the captives, and recovering of sight to the blind, to set at liberty those who are oppressed, to proclaim the acceptable year of the Lord."

> And He closed the book and gave it back to the attendant, and sat down, and the eyes of all in the synagogue were fixed on Him. And He began to say to them, "Today this Scripture has been fulfilled in your hearing."

Here it is worth noting that when Jesus speaks about the poor, the blind, the captives, and the oppressed, he is not just speaking metaphorically about the *spiritually* poor and the *spiritually* blind, or those *spiritually* captive or oppressed by the devil. He was actually reading a passage from Isaiah 61 that everyone in that synagogue would have understood was a prophecy of the work of the Messiah, and the Messiah was expected to usher in God's Kingdom, God's *shalom*, God's reign, in every respect (not just in its spiritual dimensions). The Kingdom is truly dawning on earth wherever God reigns over human minds in faith, over human wills in love, over human hearts with hope, over human bodies in health and wholeness, and over human communities with justice and peace. If Jesus had meant to overthrow those expectations completely, in favor of a solely spiritual or completely otherworldly concept of the Kingdom, He surely would have said so. Besides, we see these very this-worldly things beginning to happen in His own ministry on earth, as St. Luke makes clear in another gospel passage (Luke 7: 20-23):

> And when the [messengers from John the Baptist] had come to [Jesus], they said "John the Baptist has sent us to you saying, 'Are you He who is to come, or shall we look for another?'" In that hour He cured many of diseases and plagues and evil spirits, and on many that were blind He bestowed sight. And He answered them, "Go and tell John what you have seen and heard: the blind receive their sight, the lame walk, lepers are cleansed, and the deaf hear, the dead are raised up, the poor have good news preached to them. And blessed is he who takes no offense at me."

The "preferential option for the poor," therefore, involves a special concern for the plight of all those who are most vulnerable, or who suffer grievously in any way: those who are emotionally, morally or spiritually poor, as well as those who are physically weak or impoverished, and socially disadvantaged — and the principle applies especially to the most innocent and helpless among us. As St. John Paul II once said:

> The Christian view is that human beings are to be valued for what they are, not for what they have. In loving the poor and serving those in whatever need, the Church seeks above all to respect and heal their human dignity. The aim of Christian solidarity and service is to defend and promote, in the name of Jesus Christ, the dignity and fundamental human rights of every person.[7]

---

[7] Pope John Paul II, Address at San Antonio, September 13, 1987, cited in *The Wisdom of John Paul II* (New York: Vintage Books, 2001), p. 9.

This principle of the preferential option for the poor presents us today with a challenge. As Catholics and as citizens, we need to ask how the policies being pursued by our political leaders, our corporate leaders, and our union leaders, are having an impact on the poorest, most vulnerable members of our society. They should be our first concern in the realm of economics and politics, our "preferential" concern.

Above all they should be our preferential concern because they are first in priority for Jesus Christ. He has a compassionate bond with all those who suffer in any way, for He Himself knows what it is to be weak and helpless as an infant, to flee with his family as a refugee to a foreign land, to live in poverty as a penniless preacher and healer, with nowhere to lay His head, and finally to suffer betrayal, gross injustice and cruel death. His compassionate Heart, therefore, embraces the plight of the poor and the vulnerable in a special way, because He once shared their lot. To love them is to love Him as well, in the mystery of His Heart. Archbishop J. Peter Sartain of Seattle put it this way: "Communion with the Lord leads to deeper communion with all those loved by the Lord, especially the poor and suffering. That is the heart of Catholic social teaching."[8] Perhaps St. Theresa of Calcutta summed up the principle of Solidarity best in her teaching that there are two kinds of "real presence" of Jesus in the world: His real presence for us in the Blessed Sacrament, where He gives us His light, His life, and His love, and His real presence in the poor, where He is waiting for us to give Him back His light, His life, and His love.[9]

---

[8] Cited in Brandon Vogt, *Saints and Social Justice: A Guide to Changing the World* (Huntington, IN: Our Sunday Visitor Publishing, 2014), p. 11.

[9] See David Scott, "Mother Teresa, and Loving the Christ We Pass By" at https://catholicexchange.com/mother-teresa-loving-christ-pass .

Subsidiarity: The Preferential Option for the Family, the Local, and the Voluntary

At the same time, Solidarity always must be coupled with a third basic social precept: the principle of Subsidiarity.[10] This principle states that *the higher, more central authorities of society — and the central offices of government above all — must not usurp the role of what the Compendium calls "the original expressions of social life," especially the role of the family, and the role of voluntary associations and local social groupings of all kinds.* We can call this "the preferential option for the family, the local and the voluntary."[11]

Pope Pius XI discussed this principle in his encyclical *Quadragesimo Anno* (On the Reconstruction of the Social Order) issued in 1931 during the Great Depression, a time when there was a huge push for central governments around the world to take over the control and supervision of every aspect of life in order to "set things right" — and the most direct result of that social movement, of course, was the rise of Fascism in Europe. Here is what Pius XI wrote (quoted in the *Compendium* entry 186): "Just as it is grossly wrong to take from individuals what they can accomplish by their own initiative and industry, and give it to the community, so it is also an injustice, and at the same time a great evil and disturbance of right order, to assign to a greater and higher organization what lesser and subordinate organizations can already do."

In other words: we are indeed our brother's keeper, but central, distant authorities, and especially central government authorities, are only our brother's keeper of last resort. The

---

[10] See *Compendium*, entries 185-188
[11] That's my own summary definition — not one used by the Church in her official documents.

main work of practicing Solidarity is to be accomplished by individuals, families, churches, voluntary organizations and private charities, local businesses and local unions, and even local levels of government, not primarily by the central authorities of the State. Given that the State is the institution that by right, and according to good civic order, has a monopoly on the exercise of coercive power and compulsion (through the law, the courts, and the police forces) nothing is more dangerous to liberty, and to human rights in general, than the concentration of that coercive power in the hands of the central government — and as history has repeatedly shown, nothing is more often abused.

As Lord Acton famously said, "power corrupts, and absolute power corrupts absolutely"— although in reality, due to the universal corruption of humanity by original sin, it is not really social power that corrupts our government leaders. When that power lacks sufficient restraints (such as proper democratic and constitutional checks and balances) it simply unleashes the lust for power and dominance lurking in every human heart. Besides, families, local charities and local governments are closest to the people they serve: they know the needs of the people involved most directly, and so they can generally respond most personally, flexibly, and effectively to those needs. Notice that in St. Luke's gospel, as in all four gospels, there is no evidence that Jesus envisioned the exercise of central government power as a major factor in the dawning of the Kingdom of God "on earth as it is in heaven."

Of course, there are circumstances in which central authorities may and should intervene in local affairs and in the affairs of subsidiary groups, in what the *Compendium* calls "exceptional situations" (entry 188), to rectify grave social injustices. One thinks, for example, of the struggle to end segregation in the American South. Moreover, there is often a need for central government to insure that local areas do not lack the financial means properly to care for their poor, sick, elderly and unemployed. In general, however, central authorities are to serve and support the role of families, voluntary associations and local communities, not to supplant them, and certainly not to tyrannize over them.

The Church also teaches that it is wrong to practice Solidarity and the preferential option for the poor in ways that rob them of what the *Compendium* in entry 195 terms "the spirit of initiative," which it calls the fundamental basis of all economic and social development. In other words, except for cases of emergency aid, care for poor communities does not consist in making them perpetually dependent on hand-outs. To use the old metaphor: the best thing to do is not endlessly give them fish, but rather, teach them to fish for themselves, and provide them with rods and reels so they can catch their own fish. Thus, the best way to fight poverty is not so much to redistribute the wealth produced and owned by others (although almost any effective form of aid will involve a degree of transfer of resources); rather, the best way — the way that promotes the human dignity of the poor and provides a lasting solution to their poverty — is to enable them to produce their own sufficient supply of goods for themselves.

This, too, is implicit in St. Luke's gospel: in Christ's application of the Jubilee Year provisions to His own ministry, and to the Messianic Kingdom. In Luke chapter 4, as we have seen, Jesus quoted from Isaiah 61 that He has come to "proclaim the acceptable year of the Lord." In Isaiah this was clearly an allusion to the Jubilee Year established by the Mosaic law (see Leviticus 25), a jubilee that was supposed to happen once every 50 years in ancient Israelite society when those who were in slavery because of their debts would be released, and all lands would be returned to their ancestral, family owners (in case those lands had been lost through poverty and debt in the meantime).

The Jubilee Year provisions in the Old Testament have often been portrayed as a policy of radical income redistribution, but that is surely an exaggeration. All wealth was certainly not redistributed (for example, the Jubilee laws did not apply to flocks and herds, or to fishing boats, or to shopkeepers in the cities; nor were they designed to provide equal portions of land to all families). So the Jubilee laws did not even attempt to insure what we would call today "equality of opportunity"— but they did seek to insure *sufficient opportunity*. In other words, these laws recognized that land in ancient Israel was the most fundamental resource for creating wealth, and the Jubilee laws were therefore designed to insure that every 50 years each extended family would receive back their traditional share of that resource, so that Jewish families would not be caught in a poverty trap from generation to generation. As the book of Deuteronomy says, Israel's anti-poverty laws were meant to try to make sure that "there will be no poor among you" (Dt 15:4). Moreover, this "social insurance," so to speak, was to be established by means of civic law, not just through private charities and voluntary associations.

Of course, the interplay of these two Catholic social principles, Solidarity and Subsidiarity, and their application to the complex social realities of the day, leads to legitimate debate among Catholics as to which principle is most neglected at any given time, and therefore should take precedence in any given situation. For example, in present economic circumstances, should we focus on various forms of government intervention to stimulate economic growth and to try to support and lift the poor directly (thru, for example, extending unemployment benefits and food stamps, more government subsidized education and health care?), or should we now focus instead on directly encouraging investment in the private sector in order to try to "lift all boats at once," so to speak? What is best for the common good today: tax cuts to stimulate initiative, investment and job growth in the private sector? Or government job training and job creation initiatives a (such as infrastructure projects), and anti-poverty programs? And if government intervention is deemed necessary, which level of government is best able to do it, in keeping with the principle of Subsidiarity (federal, state, or local government)? In most cases, these are difficult discernments to make, which is why they are left by the Church as matters of "prudential judgement," rather than settled for us by definitive Church teaching. Thus, Catholics who embrace the same social principles can sometimes come to very different conclusions as to how best to apply those principles in a given time and place. This also means that all Catholics have to do their homework: they have to learn the real facts on the ground about the present social situation, and not only the social principles they need to apply to those facts.

Although prudential concern for proper Solidarity and Subsidiarity is important, in their teaching document titled "Forming Consciences for Faithful Citizenship" (2007) the United States Conference of Catholic Bishops (USCCB) reminded American Catholics that *in making prudential judgments, our duty to avoid support for "intrinsic evils" (that is, gross and even life-threatening violations of the dignity of the human person) is paramount.*

The bishops made it very clear in "Faithful Citizenship" that not all issues facing Americans today are of equal value, In section 37 of their document they wrote: "In making decisions, it is essential for Catholics to be guided by a well-formed conscience that recognizes that all issues do not carry the same moral weight," and they specifically emphasize "the special claim on our consciences and actions" of "the moral obligation to oppose intrinsically evil acts." Section 42 is particularly striking:

> As Catholics we are not single-issue voters. A candidate's position on a single issue is not sufficient grounds for a voter's support. Yet a candidate's position on a single issue that involves an intrinsic evil such as support for legal abortion or racism may legitimately lead a voter to disqualify a candidate from receiving support.

One of the things that made the 2016 presidential election in the United States so agonizing for many Catholic voters was that, arguably, both candidates at the time were advocating "intrinsic evils": Secretary Clinton with her strong support for abortion rights, the legalized killing of unborn children (something she would have secured for a generation to come through Supreme Court appointments) and Mr. Trump with his original pledge to forcibly deport all 12 million poor, undocumented (mostly Hispanic) immigrants — men, women and children.[12] This made the prudential judgment of who to vote for in 2016 very difficult indeed. It's no wonder that the Catholic vote split almost evenly between these two, deeply flawed candidates.

---

[12] I take it as given here that deporting destitute people back to lands of dire poverty can be a life-threatening violation of the dignity of human persons. This does not automatically give refugees or illegal immigrants a legal or moral right permanently to reside in the countries to which they fled — that right would be contingent upon the realistic capacity of the host country to receive them — but it does lay upon the host country the duty in charity at least to provide humanitarian assistance to such homeless, poverty-stricken people until such time as a dignified destination can be offered to them.

Catholicism and Thinking "Out of the Box"

One of the really exciting things about Catholic Social Teaching is that it often calls us to think "out of the box" of what our political parties are proposing on the social and economic issues of the day.

Ever since the 19th century, the western world has been polarized between two equally unpalatable options.

First there is socialism, in its various forms. Socialism tells us that we should turn to the government to plan a productive economy and overcome poverty. So our elected officials establish a government bureaucracy that owns and operates, or at least closely regulates and supervises the nation's industries, invests in new technologies, attempts to provide health care for us, educate our children, protect the environment, and care for the poor and the elderly. No doubt government at various levels does have a significant role to play in some of these areas, such as funding and insuring a dignified "safety-net" so that the sick, the elderly, and the unemployed do not fall into grinding poverty and destitution (an intention similar to the Jubilee laws). Moreover, the protection of workers from gross exploitation (through establishing minimum wages and maximum hours, and health and safety regulations), the prevention of concentrated economic power in the form of corporate monopolies (through anti-trust legislation), and the protection of our natural environment from reckless corporate exploitation and pollution, are generally held by most Catholics to be legitimate and helpful areas of government intervention.

Nevertheless, the Church has repeatedly condemned both communism, and even "moderate socialism"[13] as a systematic violation of the principle of Subsidiarity: for example, it is a threat to the "spirit of initiative" so vital to the production of wealth by the economy as a whole, and to lifting people out of poverty in a lasting way; and it is a danger to human rights, through the concentration of so much social and economic power in the hands of the State.

Arguably, the historical track-record of socialism bears out these concerns. From the Soviet Union in the 20th century, to Cuba, North Korea and Venezuela today, socialism has been a miserable failure, both in eradicating poverty and protecting human rights. Ironically, it does not even succeed in establishing greater social equality. Fulton Sheen explains why:

> [T]here are two serious defects among dozens of others in the Communist solution ... First, it destroys freedom.

---

[13] Pope Pius XI in *Quadragesimo Anno* (On the Reconstruction of the Social Order) defined this form of socialism as the attempt to achieve the principal goals of socialism — public ownership of the means of production and radical equalization of income — in peaceful, non-revolutionary ways that respect public order. At the time, this would have been called "Democratic Socialism." It should not be supposed, however, that the Church necessarily has condemned every social movement that labels itself "Democratic Socialism," for sometimes this label has been used for movements that seek to nationalize only public utilities and services (e.g., railroads and power companies, health and education services) while leaving the rest of the market economy intact (of course, the Church would rightly object to the nationalization or elimination of Catholic schools and colleges). Nor would every attempt to lessen income inequality necessarily contradict the teachings of Pope Pius XI. Nevertheless, all forms of socialism run a high risk of gross violations of the principle of subsidiarity.

Secondly, it does not, as it claims, destroy inequality but on the contrary creates new and worse forms of it. ...

It is quite true that Communism does away with the inequalities of wealth, because the State owns all the means of production; but in their place it has created inequalities of privilege. There are no more Big Bankers, but there are Red Leaders; there are no more Capitalists, but there are Commissars. ...

Under Capitalism it is personal wealth that produces inequalities, under Communism it is the personal control of that confiscated wealth which produces the new inequalities.[14]

Second, and at the opposite extreme, there is free-market capitalism and libertarianism in its various forms, which basically tells us that "government is best which governs least," and that the unfettered production and exchange of goods and services, with everyone permitted to pursue their own self-interest, will generally lead to liberty and prosperity for all.

No doubt the market is indeed an extraordinarily efficient mechanism for the overall production of wealth and the advance of technology — that has been more or less proven over the past few centuries, and Pope St. John Paul II said as much in his social encyclical *Centesimus Annus* (On the Hundredth Anniversary of Rerum Novarum, 1981).[15] But as the Holy Father also pointed out, it still leaves many vulnerable and underprivileged people far behind in the *distribution* of wealth (such as those lacking good educational

---

[14] Sheen, *Justice and Charity*, p. 39 and 42-43.
[15] See, for example, the careful endorsement of market economies, with many caveats, in sections 32-34 of this papal encyclical.

and job opportunities, as well as the elderly and the chronically ill). In other words, all those who are not able to be significant wealth producers are left in a poverty trap. (Again, think of the Jubilee which Christ proclaimed as part of the Kingdom He was ushering in as God's Messiah — the Old Testament Jubilee laws were designed precisely to prevent the creation of a poverty-trap in ancient Israel). As someone once wisely said: the trouble with laissez-faire, "trickle-down economics" is that it works: what makes it "all the way down" to the poor is not more than a "trickle"!

That is why the Church has repeatedly condemned laissez-faire capitalism as a general violation of the principle of Solidarity — and the track record of such forms of capitalism when they have been given full and free reign, such as in 19th and early 20th century Britain and America (and some would argue, in many places of the world from the 1980s until the Great recession of 2008), tends to bear out these concerns. As Fulton Sheen put it:

> How do we begin reconstructing the social order? ... Capitalism said: Start with liberty, understanding by liberty absence of constraint. Capitalism had its liberty and it produced unjustified inequalities, the concentration of wealth and power in the hands of a few, and the general impoverishment of the masses.[16]

The Catholic Church has encouraged us to settle for neither of these social ideologies. Unfortunately, rather than listen to the Church, over the past century or so the western world has just bounced back and forth between these options: as soon as the ills of one system and ideology begin to take hold, there is a reaction at the ballot box and the pendulum swings to the

---

[16] Sheen, *Justice and Charity*, p. 35.

other one, until the ills of that system too are clearly seen — at which point we ricochet back the other way.

It would be false, however, to say that the Church merely recommends a kind of "golden mean" between these two extremes, a "middle way" between socialism and laissez-fair capitalism (although a centrist *via media* generally violates Catholic social principles far less than the full embrace of either of these two rival systems). Rather, what the Church often seems to do is call us to think "out of the box" of this stale social debate altogether. She calls us to utilize to the full the three main social principles that we have already discussed: the Dignity of Every Human Life, Solidarity, and Subsidiarity.

According to St. John Paul II and Benedict XVI, we should explore new forms of social organization, wealth creation and distribution that do not rely so much on stifling and oppressive government bureaucracy on the one hand, or cut-throat competition and exploitation on the other. In his encyclical *Laborem Excercens* (On Human Work, 1981), for example, Pope St. John Paul II recommended trying new forms of social ownership of the means of production, such as employee share ownership (that is, employees owning shares in the companies for which they work), worker representation on company governing boards, and new forms of fairer wealth distribution that do not involve direct government intervention, such as profit-sharing arrangements. In his social encyclical *Caritas in Veritate* (Charity in Truth, 2009) Pope Benedict XVI also called on private corporations to take responsibility for helping to address some of the glaring social and economic ills in areas which they operate, especially in third world countries and poor communities.

In other words, what the world really needs is more an "economy of communion" (to employ Chiara Lubich's phrase) — *an economy of authentic cooperation among free and dignified persons* — rather than an economy primarily of public control or private competition.

Still, even the best social arrangements, however well-intentioned, will gradually self-destruct if the people within them are lacking in virtue, and living far from the grace of God. Many of those reading this book will have had direct, personal experience of exactly what I mean: the sad experience of serving on a volunteer governing committee of a club, or a charity, or a homeowners association or a local school board, and watching what should have been a cooperative effort for the common good collapse under the weight of personal jealousies and petty ambitions, indolence and indifference, nepotism and vanity, and seemingly endless bickering. An "economy of communion" is a pipe-dream if the people within it are not people of prayer, leaning on the grace of God, and striving for virtue and holiness. That is why, again (going back to the very first page of this chapter), deeper conversion and piety on the one hand, and the quest for greater social justice on the other, are inseparable. In the long run, you cannot have one without the other.

Furthermore, the gross neglect of any of the three main Catholic social principles (Solidarity, Subsidiarity or the Dignity of Persons) will lead to all sorts of social and economic miseries (and in many places, already has). All Catholics have a responsibility at least to pray, petition, and vote to prevent these social ills from spreading. As Pope St. John Paul II once wrote in his Post-Synodal Apostolic Exhortation on the apostolate of the laity, *Christifideles Laici* (On the Vocation and Mission of the Lay Faithful, 1988):

> The lay faithful should take an active, conscientious, and responsible part in the mission of the Church, in this great moment of history. A new state of affairs, both in the Church and in economic, social, political and cultural life,

calls with a particular urgency for the action of the lay faithful. If lack of commitment is always unacceptable, the present situation renders it even more so: it is not permissible for anyone to remain idle. (section 3)

A Warning from Pope St. John Paul II: Seeking Social Justice is Not Enough

By now the reader will be well aware that it is easier to see the connection between Divine Mercy and social justice than it was to see the harmony between mercy and other forms of "justice" discussed in the previous chapters of this book. As we saw in Chapter Four, it certainly stretches our minds to comprehend how a soul eternally lost in hell is also, at the same time, the object of Divine Love. If God is perfectly merciful and perfectly just in all that He is and does, however, then it must be so.

In the first chapter of this book, we said that Divine Mercy is the attribute through which God seeks to meet the needs and overcome the miseries of all of His creatures. In other words, Divine Mercy is Divine Compassion in action. And what could be more compassionate than for our merciful Lord to relieve the miseries of the sick, the poor, and the persecuted, refugees, asylum seekers and immigrants, the elderly, the unborn, and the terminally ill through the hearts and hands of His disciples? Our own merciful love just needs to be a reflection and channel of His — and few things are more merciful than to insure just and fair social treatment for everyone, in special solidarity with those most in need.

And yet, sadly enough, western civilization has a long track record of violating the call to merciful love for all while engaged in the zealous pursuit of social justice. Consider what I wrote in an article on Catholicism and Feminism for the Divine Mercy website in 2018:

> [S]ecular Feminism has become yet another chapter in the long, bloody saga of the search for social "equality" on the basis of violence. From the Reign of Terror in France in search of *civic* equality, to the Marxist revolutions and Communist tyrannies established to enforce an artificial economic equality, we can now add the social pressure put on women today to kill their own unborn children in a quest for *sexual* equality.[17]

It was considerations such as these that led Pope St. John Paul II to warn us in his encyclical on Divine Mercy, *Dives in Misericordia* (Rich in Mercy, 1980), that zeal for establishing social justice is not enough. All too often it can be used to justify slander, persecution, and even violence against those who are perceived to be perpetuating social injustices — even persecution of those who simply cannot (in good conscience) support popular proposals for attempting to rectify those injustices. In pursuit of a particular vision of social justice, whether from the left or from the right, the temptation is to become willing along the way to violate the human rights and dignity of those who do not agree. In such cases, mercy is sacrificed for the sake of justice — which, ironically, results in the loss of justice as well. Saint John Paul II explained this in his encyclical, regarding in particular the world situation in the 1980s:

> It is not difficult to see that in the modern world the sense of justice has been reawakening on a vast scale; and without doubt this emphasizes that which goes against justice in relationships between individuals, social groups and "classes," between individual peoples and states, and

---

[17] See my article "The Feminine Genius and a Civilization in Crisis" at https://www.thedivinemercy.org/news/story.php?NID=8017.

finally between whole political systems, indeed between what are called "worlds." This deep and varied trend, at the basis of which the contemporary human conscience has placed justice, gives proof of the ethical character of the tensions and struggles pervading the world.

The Church shares with the people of our time this profound and ardent desire for a life which is just in every aspect, nor does she fail to examine the various aspects of the sort of justice that the life of people and society demands. This is confirmed by the field of Catholic social doctrine, greatly developed in the course of the last century. On the lines of this teaching proceed the education and formation of human consciences in the spirit of justice, and also individual undertakings, especially in the sphere of the apostolate of the laity, which are developing in precisely this spirit.

And yet, it would be difficult not to notice that very often programs which start from the idea of justice and which ought to assist its fulfillment among individuals, groups and human societies, in practice suffer from distortions. Although they continue to appeal to the idea of justice, nevertheless experience shows that other negative forces have gained the upper hand over justice, such as spite, hatred and even cruelty. In such cases, the desire to annihilate the enemy, limit his freedom, or even force him into total dependence, becomes the fundamental motive for action; and this contrasts with the essence of justice, which by its nature tends to establish equality and harmony between the parties in conflict. This kind of abuse of the idea of justice and the practical distortion of it show how far human action can deviate from justice itself, even when it is being undertaken in the name of justice. Not in vain did Christ challenge His listeners, faithful to the doctrine of the Old Testament, for their attitude which was manifested in the words: "An eye for an eye and a tooth for a tooth." This was the form of distortion of justice at that time; and today's forms continue to be modeled on it. It is obvious, in fact, that in the name of an alleged justice (for example, historical justice or class justice) the neighbor is sometimes destroyed, killed, deprived of liberty or stripped of fundamental human rights. The experience of the past and of our own time demonstrates that justice alone is not enough, that it can even lead to the negation and destruction of itself, if that deeper power, which is love, is not allowed to shape human life in its various dimensions. It has been precisely historical experience that, among other things, has led to the formulation of the saying: summum *ius, summa iniuria* [The greater the justice, the greater the injury]. This statement does not detract from the value of justice and does not minimize the significance of the order that is based upon it; it only indicates, under another aspect, the need to draw from the powers of the spirit which condition the very order of justice, powers which are still more profound. (*Dives in Misericordia*, section 12)

The Preferential Option for Peace

This brings us to the fourth and final absolutely essential Catholic social principle (and here again I am going to give it my own label, rather than using one from the *Compendium*): the principle of "the preferential option for peace" (I just thought it might make a nice match for the other "preferential options" we have discussed so far!). In a nutshell, this principle states that *in any and every conflict situation between human communities, the Church obliges us to seek first of all, and above all, for non-violent and non-coercive ways of resolving the conflict, where such ways can be found, for this is most in accord with the dignity of every human life.* Resort to the use of force, therefore, must always be a last resort, when all other means of resolving a conflict would clearly be impractical and ineffective. If prayer, patience, dialogue, diplomacy, or even lesser forms of pressure such as formal rebuke, or diplomatic and economic sanctions can be sufficient to stop an aggressor from committing a grievous injustice, then such measures are to be preferred to recourse to arms and the horrors of war. Again, as St. John Paul II reminded us, to fight against injustice in a *merciless* manner can never be morally justified, and only leads to further violations of human rights and human dignity.

One way to think "out of the box" on issues of social conflict is to search for creative ways in which one can non-violently confront aggressors with what they are doing, and the unjust systems they are upholding. One thinks, for example, of the Non-Violent Direct Action (in the form of fasts, marches and boycotts) propagated by Mahatma Gandhi in the struggle for India's independence, and the marches and sit-ins led by Martin Luther King Jr. in the US Civil Rights movement. These non-violent gestures were meant to express a refusal to tolerate an unjust status quo any longer. The violence that the protestors suffered in response only served to highlight the hatred and injustice of those trying to preserve that status quo — hopefully drawing even the perpetrators of injustice into a new moral and social awareness.

Jesus himself taught something similar in the gospels, at least with regard to personal relationships, when he told us to "turn the other cheek" (Lk 1:29). We do not really understand this saying if we fail to take into account the cultural context here. Anglican New Testament scholar Marcus Borg neatly summarized it for us:

> [Jesus says]: "But if anyone strikes you on the right cheek, turn the other also"(NRSV). The specification of the right cheek, and the awareness that people in that world used their right hand to strike somebody provides the key for

understanding the saying. How can a person be hit on the right cheek by a right handed person? Only by a back-handed slap (act it out and see for yourself). In that world, a slap with the back of the hand was the way a superior struck a subordinate. The saying thus presupposes a situation of domination: a peasant being back-handed by a steward or official, a prisoner being back-handed by a jailer, and so forth. When that happens, turn the other cheek. What would be the effect of that? The beating could continue only if the superior used a [forehand] blow — which is the way an equal struck another equal. Of course, he might do so. But he would momentarily be discombobulated, and the subordinate would be asserting his equality even if the beating did continue"[18]

Needless to say, "turning the cheek" and other forms of non-violent protest are unlikely to be very effective in some social conflict situations — most especially in situations of conflict between nation-states, and there is no indication that Jesus insisted on the principle being applied at that level. There are some violent aggressors (e.g., dictatorial regimes bent on military conquest, or terrorists) who are just "too far gone," — too enslaved to the powers of darkness — to respond positively to non-violent gestures. That is why the Church's position on the promotion of peace is not pacifism, and not "peace at any price." The *Catechism* clearly teaches that we have a right to defend ourselves (we do not always have to exercise that right, but we do have that right), and we even have a duty in charity to defend the innocent and relatively helpless — that is, those that cannot defend themselves — from unjust aggression. If an aggressor is truly relentless, and non-coercive and non-violent means cannot or would not avail to stop them, then states have a duty, the *Catechism* says, to intervene, even militarily if necessary, to stop the spread of

---

[18] Borg, *Jesus*, p. 249.

grievous injustice and attacks on the dignity of human life. This is the Catholic doctrine of a "Just War," which the *Compendium* sums up this way in an entry titled "Legitimate Defence" (entry 500):

A war of aggression is intrinsically immoral. In the tragic case where such a war breaks out, leaders of the State that has been attacked have the right and the duty to organize a defence even using the force of arms. To be licit, the use of force must correspond to certain strict conditions: "the damage inflicted by the aggressor on the nation or community of nations must be lasting, grave and certain; all other means of putting an end to it must have been shown to be impractical or ineffective; there must be serious prospects of success; the use of arms must not produce evils and disorders graver than the evil to be eliminated. The power of modern means of destruction weighs very heavily in evaluating this condition. These are the traditional elements enumerated in what is called the 'just war' doctrine. The evaluation of these conditions for moral legitimacy belongs to the prudential judgment of those who have responsibility for the common good."

If this responsibility justifies the possession of sufficient means to exercise this right to defence, States still have the obligation to do everything possible "to ensure that the conditions of peace exist, not only within their own territory but throughout the world." It is important to remember that "it is one thing to wage a war of self-defence; it is quite another to seek to impose domination on another nation. The possession of war potential does not justify the use of force for political or military objectives. Nor does the mere fact that war has unfortunately broken out mean that all is fair between the warring parties."[19]

The principle of "the preferential option for peace," therefore, means that recourse to arms must always be a last resort, because even when it succeeds in stopping a grievous and unjust aggression, it still leaves in its wake sufferings and miseries of all kinds, sometimes even sufferings that can sow the seeds of future conflicts. So at best, taking up arms as an act of legitimate defense is what we might call "damage control" — it is not a lasting solution to the underlying problems of the world community.

In a world full of sin and rebellion against God's *shalom*, however, such "damage control" often has to be undertaken, and always at the cost of great self-sacrifice by those in the armed forces. Personally, I would argue that it was legitimately done (albeit with some moral imperfections and moral failures along the way), in some of the conflict situations over the past 75 years involving the United States; for example:

• in World War II, to stop the conquests of Hitler, and the horrific spread of Nazi tyranny and genocide;

• in the Korean War, to keep the people of South Korea from being gobbled up by the Communist tyrants of the North;

• in the first Iraq war in the 1980s, when the dictator Saddam Hussein invaded and brutalized Kuwait, and threatened the world's oil supply;

• in the Balkans in the 1990s, in the Allied effort to stop the brutal massacres (the "ethnic cleansing") perpetrated by

---

[19] See also *Catechism*, entries 2302-2317.

Serbian forces — a military intervention actually called for by Pope St. John Paul II;

• in the Afghan war, to dismantle the state-sponsored terrorism that led to the 9-11 attacks in the United States;

• and in the Allied air campaign to stop the spread of tyranny and terrorism in the Middle East by ISIS.

Of course, there is room for disagreement among Catholics about the moral legitimacy of the recourse to arms in particular cases — even about the cases I just mentioned. The principle of "the preferential option for peace," which includes the principle of "legitimate defense," will be variously applied by people of good-will, depending upon what they perceive the facts on the ground to be.

Again, the important thing for Catholics to do is to pray and ask for guidance, to understand the principles taught by the Church regarding war and peace, to learn the facts about conflict situations, and then to use their voice and their votes to stand up for the preferential option for peace in the world, a world which is a veritable powder-keg of potentially violent conflicts. According to St. Luke's Gospel, in the song the angels sang to the shepherds on Christmas eve, God is truly "glorified," and "peace on earth" only comes to people of "good-will" — not to those consumed with hatred, lust for power, or thirst for revenge.

Perhaps the story of the Nativity of our Lord, in the form that is unique to St. Luke's gospel, is the best place for us to finish this chapter. For the way Luke unfolds the great mystery of the coming of Christ, it is clear that the true Lord and Savior of the world is not Caesar Augustus, who was also called "Son of God" and "Savior of the World" in his day, and who had the centralized government power to order all the people of the Empire to be enrolled for taxation. Rather, as the angels sang, we shall find the one who is truly "the Savior, Christ the Lord ... wrapped in swaddling clothes, and lying in a manger" (Lk 2:13). And the armies that bring about the dawning of God's Kingdom in the world are the armies of angels serving and praising the birth of the Messiah, and the multitudes of disciples and missionaries He later sends out in the book of Acts to proclaim and live the gospel "in Jerusalem and in all Judea and Samaria and to the end of the earth"(Acts 1:8) — not the violent, world conquering Roman legions. And the one whose coming the angels herald was sent first of all to the poor, to a young peasant woman and a carpenter, and to shepherds abiding in the fields in the rural backwater of Bethlehem (Lk 2:8), not to the wealthy and the powerful in the palaces and courts of the Roman Empire; for as Mary sang: "he has scattered the proud in the imagination of their hearts, he has put down the mighty from their thrones, and exalted those of low degree; he has filled the hungry with good things, and the rich he has sent empty away" (Lk 1:51-53) — and he has done so not by leading a violent revolution, or by putting forward a social utopian ideal, but (among other things) by the preaching and practice of the Dignity of Every Human Life, Solidarity and Subsidiarity, and by calling his followers to do the same.

Appendix A:
Pope Francis on Divine Mercy and Divine Justice
From the Papal Bull Misericordiae Vultus (2015)
The Bull of Indiction of the Extraordinary Jubilee of Mercy

Mercy is not opposed to justice but rather expresses God's way of reaching out to the sinner, offering him a new chance to look at himself, convert, and believe. The experience of the prophet Hosea can help us see the way in which mercy surpasses justice. The era in which the prophet lived was one of the most dramatic in the history of the Jewish people. The kingdom was tottering on the edge of destruction; the people had not remained faithful to the covenant; they had wandered from God and lost the faith of their forefathers. According to human logic, it seems reasonable for God to think of rejecting an unfaithful people; they had not observed their pact with God and therefore deserved just punishment: in other words, exile. The prophet's words attest to this: "They shall not return to the land of Egypt, and Assyria shall be their king, because they have refused to return to me" (Hos 11:5). And yet, after this invocation of justice, the prophet radically changes his speech and reveals the true face of God: "How can I give you up, O Ephraim! How can I hand you over, O Israel! How can I make you like Admah! How can I treat you like Zeboiim! My heart recoils within me, my compassion grows warm and tender. I will not execute my fierce anger, I will not again destroy Ephraim; for I am God and not man, the Holy One in your midst, and I will not come to destroy" (11:8-9). Saint Augustine, almost as if he were commenting on these words of the prophet, says: "It is easier for God to hold back anger than mercy." And so it is. God's anger lasts but a moment, his mercy forever.

If God limited himself to only justice, he would cease to be God, and would instead be like human beings who ask merely that the law be respected. But mere justice is not enough. Experience shows that an appeal to justice alone will result in its destruction. This is why God goes beyond justice with his mercy and forgiveness. Yet this does not mean that justice should be devalued or rendered superfluous. On the contrary: anyone who makes a mistake must pay the price. However, this is just the beginning of conversion, not its end, because one begins to feel the tenderness and mercy of God. God does not deny justice. He rather envelopes it and surpasses it with an even greater event in which we experience love as the foundation of true justice. We must pay close attention to what Saint Paul says if we want to avoid making the same mistake for which he reproaches the Jews of his time: "For, being ignorant of the righteousness that comes from God, and seeking to establish their own, they did not submit to God's righteousness. For Christ is the end of the law, that everyone who has faith may be justified" (Rom 10:3-4). God's justice is his mercy given to everyone as a grace that flows from the death and resurrection of Jesus Christ. Thus the Cross of Christ is God's judgement on all of us and on the whole world, because through it he offers us the certitude of love and new life. (section 21)

Appendix B:
Can Divine Mercy Save Those Outside the Church?
From the Divine Mercy Q and A web series,
June 8, 2017
Robert Stackpole, STD

In recent months I have received several questions about the eternal destiny of people who are sincere seekers after truth and virtue, but who cannot in good conscience accept the Catholic faith and join the Church. What happens to them when they die? Are they cut off from grace in this life and lost forever in the next because they remained outside the Catholic fold?

For example, a woman named Cheryl shared with me these concerns:

> A few years back I went on an Emmaus walk and learned about the many graces of God, which are non-denominational. ... I no longer claim [adherence to] a denomination preferring "Christian" as my faith....I don't accept the belief of those denominations that believe they are the only ones going to heaven and/or that God's grace is not given equally to all Christians. God gave Jesus and His grace to all who believe in Him and His Son Jesus Christ.

A man named Francis also wondered what happened to those who died before the crucifixion of Christ, the birth of the Church after Easter and the spread of the Gospel. How could those people be saved? For example, he wrote, our Lord said to St. Faustina, commenting on His death at the three o'clock hour:

At that moment mercy was opened wide for the whole world (Diary, entry 1572). What does this mean for those who died before 3 p.m. on Good Friday? For as we know, many generations of people lived and died before Christ even appeared on earth. What, therefore, is their relationship with the mercy that began at 3 p.m. on Good Friday?

A few years ago I wrote a column for the Q&A series called "Divine Mercy and People of Other Faiths". That column touched upon some of these issues, but in that column I was responding to a question about the extraordinary graces of Divine Mercy Sunday, and whether those graces are available to non-Catholics as well. Here I want to expand what I said in that old column, and talk about the eternal destiny of all those in honest doubt who remain outside the Church.

What About those Who Never Heard the Gospel?

First, to the question posed by Francis: What about those who lived before the coming of Christ? How could they possibly partake of the graces of salvation Jesus won for us on the Cross for all who repent and believe in Him?

The ancient Fathers of the Church, living as they did in a largely pagan world, discussed this question in considerable depth. They held to the orthodox Christian Faith that, as Jesus said, "I am the Way, the Truth, and the Life. No one comes to the Father except through Me" (Jn 14:6). Thus, the Fathers taught that apart from participating in the life of His "Body" on earth, the Church (see I Cor 12), one cannot find salvation. At the same time, they held that to participate at least to some degree in the life of Christ and the Church it is not absolutely necessary to be a "card-carrying member" of the Church. Rather, the Church of Jesus Christ existed in some sense from the beginning of the human race. All who follow the truth and commandments of God, as far as they are aware of them, are in a spiritual sense part of the one, true Church.

For example, St. Justin Martyr in the second century taught that some people who lived before the coming of Christ were really Christians because they followed the "Logos," the Divine Word or Wisdom of God, in their hearts (see Jn 1:1-13). The same Divine Person of the Trinity - the eternal Son or Logos - is both the pre-incarnate Logos, "the light who enlightens every man who comes into the world" (Jn 1:9), as well as the one who later became incarnate for us as Jesus Christ and who died for our sins on the Cross. Thus, when relatively virtuous and godly pagans followed the guidance of the pre-incarnate Logos in their hearts, they were participating, to some extent at least, in the truth and life of Christ. Saint Justin Martyr reasoned that such people would not suffer eternal loss (Apology, 1:46). This was also the view of St. Irenaeus of Lyons (Against Heresies, 4.28.2) and St. Augustine (Epistle 102, Retractions 1.13.3).

That is also one reason why the Church included in the Apostles Creed the doctrine that after his death Christ "descended into hell" [meaning: "into the realm of the dead"]. This phrase does not only mean that Jesus Christ died a real human death. It means that between His death on the Cross on Good Friday and His Resurrection on Easter Sunday morning, His soul descended to the realm of the dead, and brought the full light and life of the Gospel to the souls of the patriarchs and prophets - and also, presumably, to the relatively virtuous pagans - so that they could share in the fruits of His redemption. The Catechism of the Catholic Church explains this doctrine in entries 631-637: "In His human soul united to His divine person, the dead Christ went down to the realm of the dead. He opened heaven's gates for the just who had gone before Him" (entry 637; cf. I Peter 3:18-19, and 4:6).

In short, a God of mercy would not unjustly condemn for all eternity everyone who lived before the time of Christ or who lived outside of the reach of Christian missions and who therefore had no chance to hear the Gospel. It must be possible for people who live in a state of "invincible ignorance" of the truth of the Gospel (in other words, ignorance of the Catholic faith that is not primarily their own fault) to be saved in the end. They may not know of God's special revelation of His love and grace through Jesus Christ. They may only know God's Divine Word or Logos through His "voice within," the voice of conscience calling them to do what is right (Rom 2:14-16) and through the beauty and order of nature, "for the invisible things of Him are clearly seen through the things that are made, even His eternal power and deity" (Rom 1:19-20). The Bible says that God has not left anyone without some witness to Himself (Acts 14:17) and that the human heart can feel after Him and find Him in its very depths, even if that heart does not yet know Him by name, because "He is not far from any one of us, for in Him we live and move and have our being" (Acts 17:27-28).

God surely judges us in the end based on how we respond to the truth about Him that we can know, not according to what we cannot know. Blessed Pope Pius IX summed up the matter in 1863 in his encyclical Quanto Conficiamur Moerore:

We all know that those who suffer from invincible ignorance with regard to our holy religion, if they carefully keep the precepts of the natural law which have been written by God in the hearts of all men, if they are prepared to obey God and if they lead a virtuous and dutiful life, can by the power of divine light and grace attain eternal life. For God, who knows completely the minds and souls, the thoughts and habits of all men, will not permit, in accord with His infinite goodness and mercy, anyone who is not guilty of a voluntary fault to suffer eternal punishment.

The Catechism sums it up in entry 847:

Those who, through no fault of their own, do not know the Gospel of Christ or His Church, but who nevertheless seek God with a sincere heart, and, moved by grace, try in their actions to do His will as they know it through the dictates of their conscience - these too may achieve eternal salvation.

What About the Salvation of Members of Other Denominations?

Now, to Cheryl's question. Cheryl asked if Christians of other denominations can receive grace too, and ultimately be saved. Or is it only Catholics who receive the grace of God and make it to Heaven in the end?

The Catholic Church teaches that those who remain outside of her fold, through no real fault of their own, are not beyond the workings of divine grace. They may live beyond the reach of Catholic missions, or they may have had the Catholic faith poorly presented to them. They may have received divine grace instead from the Catholic inheritance of Protestant or Orthodox communities of faith, churches that retained elements of Catholicism (channels of grace such as the sacraments of baptism and holy matrimony, prayer and the Holy Scriptures) when they originally separated from communion with Rome.

The Orthodox churches in particular retained the apostolic succession of bishops, and all seven of the fully authentic sacraments of the Church. Given that these Christian communities to varying degrees are channels of divine grace to their members, these communities are not fully outside of the Catholic Church. They are sharing in the life of the Holy Spirit, who is the "soul" of the Body of Christ; and they are in varying degrees of "imperfect communion" with the Catholic Church. Many of their members are walking in the way of salvation, following as much light and grace as they have as best they can. In fact, a few great saints, such as St. Meletius and St. Cyprian of Carthage, almost certainly died out-of-communion with the Bishop of Rome, because of squabbles with the Holy See, so it is not only possible to be saved, it is even possible, in very rare cases, to attain sainthood in such a state!

Thus, to the first part of Cheryl's question, the answer is clearly "yes": Those who remain outside of the Catholic Church due to invincible ignorance or honest doubt about her teachings can still receive divine grace through other Christian communities and can still be saved.

However, it seems that Cheryl wants to go even farther. She wants to believe that God's grace is equally available to all Christians. She seems to suggest that it really doesn't matter what church you belong to - that all are equal paths to the same Heaven. Someone might say the same thing about other religions, too, that perhaps they are all equal paths to the same Heaven. After all, if everyone can know at least the pre-Incarnate Logos in their hearts and find salvation in that way without ever knowing about, or believing in, the Gospel of Jesus Christ, then what is the point of Christian evangelism? If everyone can be saved - non-Catholics of every kind, whether they are Christians or not - then what was the point of the last 2,000 years of Catholic missions?

The point was simple, and must never be forgotten: Those who remain outside the Catholic Church are (to varying degrees) in a state of spiritual danger! To say that they can possibly find a path to salvation is not to

say that they necessarily will, or that the way is easy. Rather, it is fraught with peril, for outside the Church they necessarily lack many great gifts and vital sources of assistance from God —such as the fullness of revealed truth, and the fullness of the means of grace for their journey — that can only be found within the Catholic Church, "the ark of salvation" founded by Jesus Christ on the "rock" of St. Peter in the See of Rome.

To be guided on your life journey by the light of the fullness of the truth that God has revealed about Himself through Jesus Christ, and to receive the aid of the fullness of the means of grace for spiritual refreshment and healing along the way, you need to go to the Church that He originally founded through His Son (in fact, that is what the Greek word "catholikos" really means: fullness, wholeness, the whole truth and all the means of grace for the whole world).

That is why so many of the saints dedicated their lives to spreading the Catholic fullness of the Gospel of Jesus Christ, even at the cost of martyrdom. And that is why Jesus Christ, after His resurrection, gave "the Great Commission" for world evangelism: "Go therefore and make all nations My disciples, baptizing them in the name of the Father, the Son, and the Holy Spirit, and teaching them to observe all that I have commanded you. For lo, I am with you always, even to the end of the world" (Mt 28:18-20). Notice the "catholic" emphasis here: they are to bring the whole truth, to all nations, until the end of time.

Jesus must have thought that getting the Catholic fullness of truth and grace to everyone was pretty important. Otherwise He never would have given this Great Commission to His disciples. He just would have said, "It really doesn't matter whether or not you have some distorted ideas about what

God is like, which might confuse and mess up your relationship with Him, or some false ideas about the path of salvation that might lead you to go around in circles, or very limited access to the sources of grace to help you on your journey. Just set out on your life journey with your fingers crossed and try your best and everything will turn out fine!"

We would hardly call Him our "Savior" if that were the approach He took!

Of course, all this does not necessarily mean that all card-carrying Catholics are necessarily better people or more grace-filled than all non-Catholics. We all know Catholics who refuse to learn in depth the truths of their faith and who do not devoutly receive the sacraments or make any real effort to cooperate with God's grace in the way they live their lives. In the eyes of God, some non-Catholics (those who have prayerfully and obediently accepted God's truth to the extent that they can discern it, and who have followed the promptings of His grace to the extent that they have access to it) are doubtless in better spiritual condition than those Catholics who have every advantage of the fullness of truth and grace, yet who squander their spiritual inheritance!

But again: Divine Mercy can be received in its fullness in this present life only in the Body of the merciful Christ on earth which, in its fullness, is the Church Jesus Christ founded on Peter and the apostles, the Catholic Church. Those who long to be "mercified" in the fullness of His grace and who really want to become saints of His merciful Heart, will always be found within the embrace of His Church, or at least journeying ever closer to her, in good conscience, as best they can.

Appendix C
The Sacrificial-Satisfaction Theory of the Atonement: an Alternative Catholic Perspective

It is only fair to mention that the Penal Substitution Theory of Christ's redeeming work that I have defended in this book is not the only way to conceive of the Atonement that Jesus accomplished for us by His life and death. Nor is it even the most prominent way that the Atonement has been understood in the Catholic theological tradition. The majority view among saints and theologians has remained closer to what is known as the "Sacrificial" or "Satisfaction" Theory of St. Thomas Aquinas. To be sure, the precise way in which Christ redeemed us has never been solemnly defined by the Church, so within certain parameters there is room for respectful disagreement here. But it's only fair to introduce to the reader this other, venerable Catholic tradition on the unity between Divine Mercy and Divine Justice in the work of our salvation

The following is an excerpt from my book The Incarnation: Rediscovering Kenotic Christology published by The Chartwell Press in 2019. I have copied it here without the extended footnotes, so as not to distract attention from the main thread of the argument. It will give the reader some indication of why I believe the Penal Substitution or Legal Theory, when combined with something called "The Merit Theory," makes more sense than the principal Catholic tradition in this regard, the Sacrificial-Satisfaction Theory. Of course, I hope that the reader will obtain a copy of that book, and explore the much more lengthy and detailed material on this question to be found there. If my arguments (below) are convincing, all well and good. If not, at least the reader will have been offered an alternative and time-honored Catholic perspective to explore.

From Part Two, Chapter Two: On Christ's Saving Work

Most Catholic theologians today still would object to the Legal [or Penal] Theory of the Atonement on the grounds that it is just not needed: a Sacrificial-Satisfaction Theory, such as the one passed down in the Catholic tradition from Aquinas, (allegedly) shows us how God can make atonement for our sins, and unite his justice and mercy in the work of our salvation, without involving the controversial notion of penal substitution. Typically, Catholic theologians will say something like this:

> While Protestants see Christ as suffering God's wrath so we don't have to, Catholics should see Christ as making to the Father a pleasing offering into which we ourselves can be incorporated through the sacraments and, with the help of God's grace, by uniting our will to that of Christ. Our Lord's perfect obedience, and his placing of God's Law of perfect love above all earthly things was a pleasing offering to God that made atonement for our sins. In other words, the divine Son made amends to the Father and restored justice by offering to God something more pleasing than our sins were displeasing: a whole human life, from cradle to grave, of faithful obedience and perfect love, even in the face of suffering and death.

I want to suggest, however, that this Sacrificial-Satisfaction Theory of the Atonement just cannot "work" for Catholic theology in the way that this view implies.

First of all, the Satisfaction Theory, all by itself, cannot establish that Jesus in any sense accomplished an act of saving "substitution" on our behalf, which the Catholic Catechism [in entry 615] tells us is part of the mystery of our redemption. Satisfaction theories claim that Jesus shares the human experience of suffering and death, which is the inevitable and natural consequence of original and actual sin upon human life (and in that sense, he shares in our "punishment" for sin) — but sharing in an experience of something with others, even in order to accomplish something on their behalf, is certainly not the same things as substituting oneself for others: substitution means suffering something for others in their place, so that they don't have to suffer it themselves. In what sense was Jesus acting as our saving "substitute" if not by bearing in our place the punishment for sin that we deserve?

One might argue that Jesus bore the depths of human affliction for us without benefit of the companionship of a divine person incarnate. He "trod the winepress alone" (Is 63:3), so to speak, so that we do not have to do so ourselves .... But if that is all that saving "substitution" means, then we are left with [an] ... unanswered question ... about the moral intelligibility of a God who, in seeking to save us, does not also seek to meet the demands of his holiness and retributive justice in the face of the moral debt of human sin. I have argued at length that this move leaves an important aspect of God's redeeming work unfulfilled, as that work is portrayed in Scripture and the ancient Tradition of the Fathers.

Second, as we have already seen in our discussion of the theories of Aquinas and [Oxford philosophical theologian Richard] Swinburne, the Satisfaction Theory seems to make Christ's actual death on the Cross, in one major respect at least, unnecessary for the forgiveness of sins and for our salvation. Here, again, is why: Their theory states that Jesus loved his Father and all of humanity with all of his Heart, perfectly fulfilling the law of love, and that he was even willing to be killed rather than compromise this love in any way. The Father was well pleased with this whole-life offering of his divine Son in human flesh. It thereby merited the removal of our moral debt to God for our sins, applying fully to those who are incorporated into Christ's life by faith, repentance, and the sacraments. No doubt all of this has elements of truth in it as far as it goes. But why, then, would Christ's actual death on the Cross be necessary? Given that he was the divine Son Incarnate, and that all his human acts are "theandric" and therefore of infinite value,[1] Christ's mere willingness to die, if it came to that, would have been enough to make his self-offering of love complete. Some of the saints have held that even the shedding of one drop of Christ's Blood would have been enough all by itself to save the world. This is the Satisfaction Theory of Aquinas and Swinburne taken to its logical conclusion. But if that is so, then surely Christ saved the world in the Garden of Gethsemane when he surrendered himself in love to the Father and sweat drops of blood! How, then, could the teaching of the 16th century Council of Trent of be true that it was "by His most holy Passion on the wood of the Cross" that Christ "merited justification for us" and "made satisfaction for us unto God the Father" [session VI, chapter seven]? And how could the teachings of Pope St. John Paul II be true that Jesus offered a just "compensation" for our sins on the Cross [Dives in Misericordia, 1980, section 7]? Jesus said to the disciples on the road to Emmaus: "Was it not necessary that the Messiah should suffer these things and enter into his glory?" (Lk 24:26) For some reason, he could only say of his saving work "It is finished" at the moment of his death, and not before (see Jn 19:30) [NB: The same word, "finished" in Greek, tetelestai, was commonly used in the Greco-Roman world to write on a bill that had been paid.

---

[1] "Theandric" means "God (*theos* in Greek) acting through a human (*andros*) vehicle": St. Thomas Aquinas used the term to indicate that everything that Jesus Christ said and did was an expression of the infinite love of God through the human nature that he assumed, and therefore everything Jesus said and did was of infinite value for our salvation.

Thus, the word could mean "finished" in the sense of "over and done with: the amount owing has been paid off."].

Typically, Catholic theologians will respond to all this that even though our Lord's crucifixion may not have been strictly necessary to save us, to pay our debt to his justice, still, it showed the magnitude of God's love for us in that he was willing to undergo such a death and make such a sacrifice. But again (as we discussed earlier in this chapter), authentic "love" can only be fully expressed in action for the benefit of another. If Christ's crucifixion was not really needed in order to save us from objective guilt and to obtain the forgiveness of our sins, then how would it express the magnitude of his "love" for us? No doubt it establishes and expresses his deepest solidarity with the afflictions of humanity — which is certainly a great act of love for us — but not in a way that directly and objectively redeems us from our sins: and it is the Cross as the locus of redemption from sin ... that is the clear witness of both Scripture and Catholic Tradition.

In short, I would argue that what made the Son's offering of himself on the Cross pleasing to the Father was that by dying on the Cross, he thereby carried to completion the loving plan of the Blessed Trinity of bearing in our place the penalty we deserve for our sins — a sacrifice really necessary to win our pardon. It was a plan that the Son willingly accepted when he was sent into the world in the first place (see Mk 10:45; Jn 3:16).

The Sacrificial-Satisfaction Theory, it would seem, just does not work in the way that Catholics have often claimed, and much that it seeks to express can be found in a different way: in a combination of the Penal Substitution and the Merit theories of Christ's saving work.

Robert Stackpole

Suppose that human "sin" against God differs radically from the moral debts we accrue from the wrongs we do to one another. The main difference would be that our sins cannot be fully "atoned for" in the very "human" way that Aquinas and Swinburne describe. In other words, suppose we cannot make sufficient "satisfaction" for sin, not even with the help of Christ, since there is nothing that we could weigh in the balance in our favor against the betrayal of the infinite love of [God] our Total Benefactor that all our sins imply. In short, suppose it just is the case that temporal punishment is due for venial sin, and both temporal and eternal punishment for mortal sin, and no amount of repentance, on its own (that is, no amount of contrition, apology, works of reparation and penance, not even devoutly offering up Christ's perfect life and death at the Eucharist), could completely cancel that debt. After all, even our works of atonement and our sacramental worship are almost always tainted by half-hearted repentance and weak faith (Rom 7:14-25; I Jn 1:8-9). And even when they are not, the full demands of justice, the "penal debt" that we owe, remains to be paid [NB: the notion of "penal debt" is explored in-depth earlier in this chapter of the book].

What we know from Scripture and Tradition is that "the wages of sin is death" (Rom 6:23), both as an inevitable consequence and as a just punishment. Thus, to betray God's infinite love (as every mortal sin does) on the scales of his justice surely deserves a relatively infinite penalty: the penalty of bodily suffering and death (the temporal punishment due for all sin) and everlasting spiritual death (the eternal punishment due for mortal sin) — that is, complete alienation from God. And by God's just ordinances from the beginning, these are also the inevitable effects (the "natural consequences," so to speak) of unrepented mortal sin on human life: the loss of the life-giving Holy Spirit, resulting in the decay and ultimate loss of both physical and spiritual life — in other words, the state of "death" from sin that St. Paul

204

describes in his letters (e.g. Rom 5:12-21). But Jesus Christ substitutes himself for us on the Cross by experiencing there in his body and soul — and thereby paying for us — the equivalent (by close analogy) of that temporal and eternal penalty, so that those who are in faithful and loving union with him do not have to pay that penalty themselves: "There is therefore now no condemnation for those who are in Christ Jesus" (Rom 8:1; cf. Gal 5:6). Our Savior's act of loving "penal substitution" takes care of our moral debt to God. When we are united to him by repentance and faith, informed by love (and to the degree that we are thus united with him), it clears our account and wins our pardon.

Nevertheless, a cancelling of debts and a full pardon for the past, on its own, still does not obtain for us all the graces that we need to be fully sanctified and prepared for everlasting life. In other words, what adequately deals with the past (on the scales of justice) does not necessarily take care of all the needs of the present and the future.

Here is where elements of the Merit Theory of Christ's saving work address our need. Jesus not only died for us: he also lived for us. From cradle to grave, he offered his whole life as one continuous act of love for his heavenly Father, and for us. Since this was an offering of a divine person in human flesh, it was a "theandric" self-sacrifice well-pleasing to the Father, and its meritorious value before the scales of Divine Justice was therefore infinite and super-abundant for its purpose (which was not to compensate Divine Justice for our sins, but to merit for us sanctifying grace). As a result, when we are spiritually united with him through authentic repentance and faith, informed by love (and to the degree that we are thus united to him), we can receive the renewal in our hearts of the life of the Holy Spirit, and all the graces we need for the sanctification of our whole life-journey, in preparation for eternal life. Indeed, by His whole-life offering, Christ has merited all the graces needed for the sanctification of the entire world and the coming of the new heavens and the new earth portrayed in the Book of Revelation (chapter 21), the Kingdom of God that abides forever.

In short, Jesus made up for our misspent past when he bore the penalty that we deserve on the Cross. He also merited for us, by his whole life and death of loving obedience to the Father, all the sanctifying graces that can heal us and set us free from sin's power in our lives. That's not just some cold, impersonal, judicial transaction. It's a wonderful gift of his mercy that sets us free from both the guilt and power of sin! All we need to do to receive that gift is to open our hearts to Jesus Christ more and more by repentance and faith.

An understanding of Christ's saving work such as this includes all that is true and helpful from the Sacrificial-Satisfaction Theory, without the added problem of making Christ's death on the Cross, in a major respect, superfluous to our redemption. Catholics could still say that in offering up the life and death of Jesus Christ to the Father at every Eucharist, we are pleading for the (penal) benefits of his Cross to be applied to our souls, and for all the sanctifying graces he merited by his life and death to be poured out upon us, and upon the whole world.

Made in USA - North Chelmsford, MA
1222385_9780991988082
01.07.2022 0849